CAPITAN
NEW MEXICO

27 May 2013

To Barbara

With best wishes

Gary W. Coffman

CAPITAN
NEW MEXICO

FROM THE COALORA COAL MINES
TO SMOKEY BEAR

GARY COZZENS

Charleston · London

THE
History
PRESS

Published by The History Press
Charleston, SC 29403
www.historypress.net

Cover images: Smokey Bear image, *David Cunningham of Smokey Bear State Park*. Titsworth
Store employee picnic, *Hollis Cummins*.
Back cover images photographed by the author.

First published 2012

Manufactured in the United States

ISBN 978.1.60949.451.3

Library of Congress Cataloging-in-Publication Data

Cozzens, Gary.
Capitan, New Mexico : from the Coalora coal mines to Smokey Bear / Gary Cozzens.
p. cm.
Includes bibliographical references and index.
ISBN 978-1-60949-451-3
1. Capitan (N.M.)--History. 2. Capitan (N.M.)--Biography. I. Title.
F804.C365C69 2012
978.9'64--dc23
2012005899

This book is respectfully dedicated to my parents,
L.C. and Mary Lou Cooper Cozzens.

CONTENTS

PREFACE

Over forty million years ago, the Sierra Blanca region of south central New Mexico experienced significant volcanic activity that lasted more than twenty million years. The result produced abundant mineral resources still being discovered and mined today. The mineral field was deposited around the shoreline of a large lake during the Mesozoic era, and volcanic activity and coal seams continued to form, especially in the Capitan area.

The resulting coal is a low-quality C bituminous coal. Mining the coal is often hampered by intrusive dikes of igneous rocks, numerous structural faults and gravel terraces that conceal any trace of the underlying coal fields.[1]

Coal was first discovered in the area in 1884, and the earliest mine was the Linderman Mine, located two miles west of Capitan. This mine supported activities at Fort Stanton beginning in 1885 and continued later when the fort became a tuberculosis sanitarium. In 1899, the New Mexico Fuel Company began large-scale coal mining, resulting in the rapid growth of both Coalora and Capitan.

The Salado Creek flows east through the Salado Flats from high ground to the west until joining the Bonito River between Capitan and Lincoln. It was near Salado Flats that Jose Padilla and his extended family, along with four laborers, had settled before 1870, as documented in the U.S. census from that year. This is the first recorded settlement of the area. Jose sold milk and butter to Fort Stanton.

Ten years later, the census shows much more settlement at Salado Flats, with fifty-seven people living in the area. Most of the people were still laborers and farmers, but now there were also blacksmiths, dairymen, carpenters and matchmakers. Among those inhabitants were Teofilo and Estanislada Lalonde,[2] who had moved to the area known as Cienaga Magado, thought to have been on the Magado Creek just south of Capitan. Estanislada "Lada" LaLonde was the daughter of Jose Padilla. About 1885, the LaLondes sold their eighty-acre ranch and moved to the Nogal area.[3]

Salado Flats, where Capitan is now located, was once a beautiful meadow producing gamma grass due to a low water table. Manuel Aguilar, a "milker," lived at the Juan Andre Silva ranch at this time.[4]

INTRODUCTION

Without a doubt, the most famous resident of Capitan was a brown bear cub. Smokey Bear was found with badly burnt paws clinging to a tree during a forest fire in May 1950. In shock and near death from his burns and dehydration, the cub quickly became the national living symbol for fire prevention. While other historical events occurred in the area during the past millennium, it was Smokey Bear who put Capitan on the map.

As with all books, many people are responsible for providing support to make this book possible. First and foremost are my parents, L.C. and Mary Lou Cooper Cozzens. Dad talked about the history of the area—that of happenings other than Smokey Bear and Billy the Kid. He spoke of Titsworth and Pfingsten and the Nogal Mesa. Moreover, he has lived ninety years of Capitan history from his time in school here, where he was a standout athlete earning twelve letters between 1937 and 1940 before attending the University of New Mexico on a basketball scholarship. He became a school administrator and ended his career as superintendent of the Capitan Schools. Mom was an elementary school teacher, and she, too, ended her career at the Capitan Schools. Both parents encouraged me to read and to learn. To them I am eternally grateful.

My paternal grandfather, Seymour "Primo" Cozzens, was also a teacher of local history, as were my uncles Wayne Cozzens, Bob Parsons and Doyle Cozzens.

It is hard to talk about the history of the Capitan area without mentioning the name of Herbert Lee Traylor. Herbert Lee was the "dean" of local historians. Also writing about the history of the Capitan area was Dorothy Guck, who holds the distinction of being the only reporter to cover the fire in which Smokey Bear was found. Following Dorothy is Roberta Key Haldane, a copious note taker who supplied much of the background material for this book and, most importantly, helped to edit it into a much better book. More recently, in 2000, Lionel W. (Lonnie) Lippman and Virginia Watson Jones published a book on the centennial of Capitan.

Hollis Cummins provided much of this history along with many historic photographs in this book. LaMoyne and Opal Peters once again shared their knowledge of the area and historic photographs, as did Wally Ferguson, Fred Kendall and Ellis and Sheryl Vickers. Barbara Jeanne Reily-Branum, a descendant of early settlers, provided detailed information and photographs. Richard Bryant once again worked wonders with the old pictures. Preston and Willa Stone, ranchers from north of the Capitan Mountains, were major contributors. Nancy Hasbrouck and her daughter, Donna Ikard, provided family photographs and a previously unpublished interview with Monroe Howard. Pam Allen helped to get pictures, and Rich Eastwood provided information on the early settlement. Carlton Britton provided information on the Block Ranch. Dick Cox, Garth Hyde, Paul Jones, Agatha Long and Gerald Dean all provided oral history of the area. Thank you to Becky LeJeune and The History Press team.

U.S. Forest Service archaeologists Diane Prather and Eric Dillingham provided much information on the Forest Service history. Additionally, I was allowed access to the Lincoln National Forest files, which proved very helpful. David Cunningham and Rebecca Judd from the Smokey Bear State Park provided information and photographs on Smokey Bear and forest activities around Capitan.

Pat Garrett and Raynene Greer at the Capitan Public Library were able to obtain books through interlibrary loan. More importantly, Ms. Garrett, along with Tiffany Menix, produced an oral history in 2006 in which elementary students collected information and interviewed locals to produce that book.

Elvis Fleming and John Lemay of the Southeast New Mexico Historical Society provided period photographs included in this book.

Finally, my greatest supporter continues to be my wife, Shirley Crawford. She is my blessing, as are our daughter, Kristi; our granddaughter, Ridley; and my mother-in-law, Erma.

CHAPTER 1

GRAY, COALORA AND THE EL PASO AND NORTHEASTERN RAILROAD

GRAY

Seaborn Gray, the founder of Capitan, was born in Coosa County, Alabama, on October 31, 1851, and was raised in Louisiana. In 1873, he married Sarah Glenn, and the couple had six children. Coming to New Mexico in 1884 at the urging of his cousin Pat Garrett, Gray worked with former Lincoln County sheriff Pat Garrett on the VV Ranch, twelve miles south of Capitan. In 1887, he moved to the Salado Flats and continued his dealings in cattle.

In 1897, he opened the first store on his ranch and was successful in establishing a post office, which he named Gray after himself. He was also instrumental in securing a railroad line, first to Coalora and then to Capitan. He owned a livery stable in 1890 and engaged in mining.[5]

Gray had been in bad health for a number of years and had previously had at least three distinct strokes. He passed away quietly one Sunday morning in 1916 with his family present and was buried in the Capitan cemetery.[6]

One of Gray's daughters, Nellie, married William Reily of Capitan, who owned a large amount of land on the north side of the village.

On September 28, 1892, Gray applied for a land patent in the area known as Salado Flats. He quickly purchased the land from the Salado Creek to the Bonito River, naming the settlement around his home Gray, and thus became the founding father of the village later called Capitan.[7]

Founded in 1894, the early settlement of Gray is sometimes erroneously called the original name for Capitan, but in fact, this small settlement was located

Seaborn T. Gray, founder of Capitan, circa 1910.
Photograph courtesy of Barbara Jean Reily-Branum.

about a mile south of the current village. Gray's ranch included a store and the post office. Gray's residence was located on this spot, but his barn and stables were where Smokey's Country Market in Capitan is located today. It was in these livery stables that the famous racehorse Steamboat was quartered for a time. Later on, Tom Key, Hart Hale and then Mosa Maryfield lived in Gray's original house. Gray was active until about 1900, when the village of Capitan was established north of the Gray site.[8]

Tom Key, from Lipan, Texas, married Ellen Green and moved to the Sacramento Mountains to homestead. In 1917, Ellen insisted the couple move to Capitan for better schooling for their children, Ernest and Hilda, and they bought the Seaborn Gray ranch south of town, owning it for the next thirty years.

Tom became a small rancher and jack-of-all-trades, including a farmer, carpenter, blacksmith, veterinarian, shoe repairman and mechanic. It was Tom Key who built the bridge over the Magado Creek where the fairgrounds are located on the old road to Nogal. Ellen tended a flock of some two thousand White Leghorn chickens and made butter from the cream of the cows on the ranch, which Tom shipped to El Paso every week with twelve-gallon kegs of cream.

Tom passed away in 1941, and Ellen lived on the ranch until about 1947 before selling it and moving into Capitan, where she died in 1966.

Their daughter Hilda married Jack Young and was a schoolteacher in Capitan for a number of years. Son Ernest went to George Washington University before returning to Lincoln County, where he served as county clerk in the 1930s. Ernest married Janie Haldeman, who had come to Capitan to teach school. Their children, Jack, Roberta and Beverly, all live in the mountains east of Albuquerque today.

Seaborn Gray homestead south of Capitan, circa 1990. Some of the original buildings are in the photograph. *Photograph courtesy of Barbara Jean Reily-Branum.*

The 1900 U.S. census showed a combined population for the area of 670, probably with most coming from Coalora. Coal continued to be mined in the area with the nearest site known as the Magado Creek Mine, operated by the New Mexico Fuel Company from about 1898 to about 1907.[9]

In 1901, the *Capitan Progress* reported:

> *The unusually large number of prairie schooners that came to anchor in this port within the past few months show plainly which way the tide of immigration is flowing and no better evidence is needed to prove that Lincoln County and Capitan are largely forging rapidly to the front. The most of these people are men with small means who are looking for a place where they can secure land cheap and build houses. As a result the countryside is becoming dotted with farms and small ranches. It is the permanent settler who makes the country and furnishes the backbone for towns, hence the future for Capitan and Lincoln County grows brighter and brighter every day.[10]*

COALORA

When coal was discovered here in 1884, the site was called Sierra Blanca Coal Field and then the Capitan Coal Field before it was named "Coalora."

In 1898, the Coalora coalmines were opened and by 1900 were producing two hundred thousand tons of coal a year with a monthly payroll of $10,000. Large coalfields were discovered in the Salado Flats, and the Akers mines were opened in 1899. Beginning in 1905, over six hundred thousand tons of coal were mined over the next decade. The coal was in two seams with the Akers Mines on the west and the Ayers Mines on the east. These mines were managed by the New Mexico Fuel Company, which ran three shifts.[11]

In 1900, the El Paso and Northeastern Railroad built a spur line from Carrizozo to Coalora to supply coal for its expanding operations. By 1902, about two thousand people resided here, mainly five hundred coal miners from Pennsylvania. At one time, the company town had a railroad station, large company store, offices, the ever-present saloon, residences for the manager and technical men, shacks for the miners and their families, a hospital, a school, a post office (1903–1905) and a doctor's office. The first boardinghouse was operated by Waverly Johnson and his wife.[12]

Because Coalora was a company town, it always had supplies but was constantly short of cash. Ethel Keathley remembers:

> "We had much to thank the coal company for. They provided a payroll, also a good market for chicken eggs, dairy products and garden truck. I wrote a letter home that said 'everything green except myself, was saleable.' I've even seen small boys sell lambs quarter, an edible weed.
>
> One drawback was that the Coalora boys were always short of ready cash—they never seemed to have a dime on them. They were eager to buy, but the stock question was: 'Will you take script?'
>
> It was the queerest medium of exchange I have ever seen. Just about everyone had some of it in their pockets and purses. I sewed a lot for miners' women folks, but was always paid in script."[13]

In September 1900, the Southwestern Mercantile Company hosted a ball for the ladies of Capitan and Lincoln County in the new store. The mercantile furnished the supplies for the ball, and the women cooked the food. Belle Stephenson was chosen "Belle of the Ball," while William Smith was voted the homeliest man. A.L. Cummings and Edith Gray won cake for being the best waltzers. Profits were donated to the Red Men, a fraternal order, to complete their hall.[14]

In 1901, the *Capitan Progress* reported:

> *North of Capitan is the coal camp and home of the miners, also the present terminus of the El Paso and Northeastern railway. It has about*

Trains hauling coal at Coalora, circa 1900. *Photograph from Roy Harmon Collection, courtesy of White Oaks Historical Association.*

> *700 inhabitants. It is like any coal camp in its long rows of red houses and its cosmopolitan population. It has an excellent hospital, fine depot, large mercantile store, and but one saloon. No more allowed by the company...There are about 300 miners in the camp, employed at 31 cents an hour.*[15]

There were two thousand reported residents in Coalora by 1902, supported by the Southwestern Mercantile Company, the Club Hotel, the New Mexico Fuel Company Hospital, Wells Fargo Express, a livery stable and one saloon. A post office was established in Coalora in 1903 but closed when the population dwindled to 350.[16]

The Akers and Ayers mines were opened by the New Mexico Fuel Company in 1899, operating under General Manager W.P. Thompson for the New Mexico Railway and Coal Company of New York City. Two beds of coal were worked at this mine. Because of their nearness to the railroad, they were inspected repeatedly. The Akers Number 1 became the Capitan No. 1 and was inspected on February 6, April 6, June 5 and November 10, 1900. The mine had "a slope depth of 800 feet, with a 3 to 6 foot vein of bituminous coal, that produced 41,260 tons of coal valued at $82,520. The No. 1 employed 85 men and boys, and was equipped with a 10 by 12 hoisting engine, 40- and 60-horsepower boilers, a 10 ft. Crawford and McCrimmon fan, and a good blacksmith shop."[17]

Located about a mile from No. 1, the Akers No. 4, later referred to as Capitan No. 2, was on the same vein. It was inspected on February 7,

Coal staged at the railroad in Coalora, circa 1900. *Photograph from Roy Harmon Collection, courtesy of White Oaks Historical Association.*

April 7, June 5 and November 10. The inspector noted that the mine had a "thickness of 2½ to 6 feet. With a slope of 850 ft., yearly production was 29,327 tons of bituminous coal valued at $58,654. The No. 4 employed 57 men had a 10 by 12 hoisting engine, a 12 ft. Crawford and Crimmon fan, an 18 by 20 Howard air compressor, and two 60-horsepower boilers."[18] Although the mine was found to be in good shape, the inspector ordered the general manager to erect a furnace in February and additional timber at No. 1 in April.

Ayers No. 2, 7 and 8 were located about three-quarters of a mile from Aker's No. 1 on a second coal seam. They were similar to No. 1 and No. 4. A tramway led from No. 7 and No. 8 to a tipple at No. 2 where the coal was loaded into railroad cars for shipment to El Paso.

The Akers mines continued to be worked in 1901, but the vein started to play out. In 1902, the inspector was referring to some of these mines as "North Capitan," probably referring to Coalora. He wrote that the town supporting the mines had "a population of 600, 100 dwellings, a good school house, 2 boardinghouses, and a company hospital."[19]

Capitan Nos. 1 and 4 were found to be in good condition in 1902, but an intensive investigation was conducted in May after falling rocks killed three miners in three weeks. In 1903, the mines were again found to be in good condition, but more timber shoring was ordered due to two deaths, one at each mine. By 1903, Lincoln County was the third-largest coal-producing county in New Mexico. [20]

Coal tipple at Coalora, circa 1900. Note shacks to the right of the photograph. *Photograph from Roy Harmon Collection, courtesy of White Oaks Historical Association.*

By 1904, the Coalora fields had played out because the coal deposits were thin and interrupted by numerous faults and dikes. The railroad stopped production at the Coalora mines in 1906 and moved its mining operation to Dawson, not far from Raton in northeast New Mexico. Production continued at a minimal rate, but the buildings were dismantled and also moved to Dawson.[21]

The year of 1905 was not a good one for coal mining in the area. The inspector noted that the population of Coalora had shrunk from five hundred in 1903 to fewer than twenty-five, the post office was closed and most of the remaining buildings were torn down and moved to another location. Capitan No. 1 was operated at a much-reduced rate, and the coal that was mined was sold to Forty Stanton. Capitan No. 2 was closed down, and the last rail shipment was made on April 27.[22]

Capitan No. 1 was abandoned in 1906. In 1910, the old Linderman mine was reopened as the Gray mine. A new slope was sunk to a depth of 250 feet, but only 250 tons of coal, valued at $750, were mined and the mine was closed.[23]

During this time, the area experienced several domestic incidents. Capitan coal miner Carpio Lobato came home and found his wife in the embrace of Catarina Mendoza. Lobato immediately killed Mendoza and then turned himself over to Deputy Sheriff W.H. Sevier. In another case, Deputy Sheriff W.M. Smith returned Joseph Noble to Capitan from Alamogordo. Noble was accused of robbing A.W. Swindel's saloon at the Linderman mine and

Coalminers on tipple at Coalora, circa 1900. *Photograph from Roy Harmon Collection, courtesy of White Oaks Historical Association.*

taking several bottles of alcohol. Several men who enjoyed the beverages with him implicated him in the crime.[24]

On June 26, 1900, John Eddy dissolved his partnership with his brother Charles due to the inability to mine coal profitably at Coalora.[25] In 1905, the railroad moved almost the whole town and its inhabitants to the new coal-mining town of Dawson. A section of Dawson in which the former Coalora residents lived was known as "Capitan." The railroad closed and abandoned the spur line to Carrizozo in 1943. No trace of this thriving little village remains today.[26]

After the closure of Coalora, coal for Fort Stanton was brought up the railroad spur line and dumped at Capitan, where it was hauled to Fort Stanton. It was reported that Fort Stanton alone required three hundred carloads of coal a year.

EL PASO AND NORTHEASTERN RAILROAD

When coal was discovered about one mile northwest of Capitan in the late 1890s, Charles B. Eddy decided the vein was rich enough to provide coal for his new El Paso and Northeastern (EP&NE) Railroad, and he built a spur line from Carrizozo to Coalora, which opened on September 29, 1899. The twenty-one-mile line ascended a 4.3 percent grade and a switchback from Carrizozo over Indian Divide to Coalora. The Lincoln

County Board of Commissioners signed a ninety-nine-year lease with Eddy for a franchise of the El Paso and Northeastern Railroad. By 1900. a railroad depot was built in Coalora, but the coal veins soon played out. The line was operated by the EP&NE Railroad until 1905, when the lease expired and the railroad operation was taken over by the El Paso and Southwestern Railroad.

The construction of the El Paso and Northeastern Railroad was announced on the front page of the *Santa Fe New Mexican* on October 21, 1897. Originally called the White Oaks Railroad, it was to run about 165 miles from El Paso north to Carrizozo. White Oaks was bypassed, and the line was renamed El Paso and Northeastern Railroad later in September 1897.[27] The track was laid starting in 1898 and reached Carrizozo by 1899. The first load of coal was shipped to El Paso on September 29, 1899.

THE CAPITAN SPUR LINE

In 1899, a spur line was built to the Coalora coalfields and later into Capitan. The line was next extended from Carrizozo to Santa Rosa as the El Paso and Rock Island Railroad Company where it connected with the Chicago, Rock Island and El Paso Railroad. Phelps Dodge bought the line in 1905, and it became the El Paso and Southwestern Railroad. In 1924, the Southern Pacific Transportation Company purchased the line. Water was supplied by a pipeline in the Sacramento Mountains from the Bonito and Nogal Lakes to the pumping station at Coyote north of Carrizozo. A roundhouse was built at Carrizozo while Capitan, Corona and Ancho had railroad depots.

In February 1901, the first train came to Capitan, and as early as 1902, stock pens were built at Capitan allowing ranchers to use the railroad. They previously had to drive their herds much farther to ship them to market. By October 1911, a more permanent stockyard was built near the Titsworth Mercantile Company at the end of the rail line.

Johnson Stearns tells about the track between Carrizozo and Coalora:

> *When you were traveling between Carrizozo and Capitan now on Highway 380 you can discern the old roadbed in many places and just west of the high point on Indian Divide you will see the switchback that enabled this little train to negotiate the grade. The train would chug forward over the*

Above: Train on the El Paso and Southwestern Railroad on the railroad spur from Carrizozo to Capitan, circa 1930. *Photograph courtesy of Johnson Stearns.*

Below: Switchback on the Capitan Spur railroad line, circa 1930s. *Photograph courtesy of Johnson Stearns.*

switch on the track they were traveling until the caboose had cleared the switch, the trainmen would get off, open that switch and the little train would back up the canyon toward the Ranchman's Camp Meeting until it reached a point where the caboose had passed over another switch and also the engine had cleared that point. The trainmen would then re-align that switch opening it up to allow them to proceed up that track to top of the hill *and on into Coalora and Capitan. At Coalora there was a wye and could turn the engine at that point for return to Carrizozo.*[28]

The train went from Carrizozo up Indian Divide to Coalora. There was a switch at Coalora where they would turn the train around to go back down the hill to Carrizozo. They would also use the switch to turn the train around to back it into Capitan since there was no way to turn the train around once it got there.[29]

THE CAPITAN DEPOT

The Coalora Depot was transported to Capitan in 1906. Moving depots on flat cars by rail was a relatively common practice in this era. The frame depots were easily moved and could be relocated to more populous locations as New Mexico's towns developed.

About the same time, George A. Titsworth purchased one-half interest in the local grocery store owned by E.B. Welch. When Coalora shut down, the railroad tried to tear up the rails but was stopped by Titsworth, who by this time had won several lucrative contracts with the Fort Stanton Marine Hospital.

Train service between Carrizozo and Capitan was inconsistent at best. Two engines were required to bring the train up the hill and over Indian Divide. Postmaster Ritter summed up the timeliness of the railroad when he commented: "I spent thirty-four years in government service in Santa Fe, and twenty years in Lincoln County with six years at Fort Stanton, four years at Lincoln and seven years at Capitan." When Ritter was asked where he spent the other three years, he replied, "Oh, the other three, I spent those at Carrizozo waiting for the train to Capitan."

In 1943, the El Paso and Northeastern tracks were finally removed to use the steel for the war effort. By this time, Titsworth's power was declining, and the Lincoln County commission allowed the railroad to refute the ninety-nine-year franchise it had signed in 1900.

The floor plan of the Capitan Depot is similar to that of many depots of the time, with a freight room on one end that is raised to facilitate loading baggage onto the raised rail cars and an agent's office/baggage room adjacent to the freight room with large double doors so that the agent could check in baggage. On the other side of the office is a ticket room, where passengers could purchase tickets through a ticket window between the two rooms, but this window has been removed in the Capitan Depot. On the

Capitan Railroad Depot, circa 1940s. The depot was originally located at Coalora but was moved to Capitan in 1905. *Photograph courtesy of Dorothy Victor.*

other side of the ticket room are the men's and ladies' waiting rooms. Each has a separate outside entrance and a separate door to the ticket room.

Marci L. Riskin describes the depot:

> *The simplified El Paso and Northeastern depot has the typical hipped, shingled roof with a generous overhang, but without a projecting agent's bay. On its main-line depots, the railroad used lapped horizontal siding with board and batten bases, but board and batten covers the entire exterior of this branch-line depot. The details are also relatively plain; an unadorned wood cornice, straight brackets, and simple two pane double hung windows rather than the more stylish vertical four pane over two seen in the Ancho and Corona depots. The plan was also simple: a waiting room on the east, an agent's office, a baggage room at street level, and a freight room at railcar level.*[30]

CHAPTER 2

CAPITAN

Capitan's name comes from the nearby Capitan Mountains, which were probably named for Captain Saturnino Baca. The U.S. census of 1900 showed its population as 670 after the railroad arrived and the town site was platted. Capitan was incorporated in 1937 with a mayor, a police department and a volunteer fire department. The centerpiece of the village was George A. Titsworth's Titsworth Mercantile Company, locally known as the Titsworth Store, an enterprise that became the vehicle for Titsworth's power and remained so until his death in 1949. The railroad closed and abandoned the spur line from Carrizozo to Capitan in 1943, and the tracks were used for the war effort.

For a long time there was no electricity in Capitan, but many of the houses and stores were wired in anticipation of it. Electricity finally arrived in the early 1930s, through a local power company. Most of the wiring was installed by Joe Wigley.

The Eddy brothers purchased Seaborn Gray's land through a business subsidiary called the Alamogordo Improvement Company, platted it and extended the railroad spur into the new village. As a result, Capitan's first lot was sold on March 4, 1900, and within one year the town had a population of one thousand people.[31]

By May 1900, the little village had grown to a point where there were

eight stores, two saloons, two jewelry shops, two lumber yards, two barber shops, two restaurants, a bakery, a hotel, a drug store, a shoemakers shop,

Above: Capitan street scene, circa 1905. The Forest Reserve Building is on the left and the Welch and Titsworth Store is next to it on the right. *Photograph courtesy of Hollis Cummins.*

Below: View of Capitan looking east above the road from Lincoln, circa 1920s. *Photograph courtesy of LaMoyne and Opal Peters.*

a meat market, a blacksmith shop, two livery stables in Capitan and all are kept busy. The new artesian well, one mile west of Capitan, forces the water through a pipe to a height of 15 feet. The water is of superior quality and is the second artesian well in the area with a depth of less than 200 feet.[32]

It is reported that by 1911, P.G. Peters had taken control of the village and raised the price of the town lots by 100 percent. Peters, an early settler in the county and a local businessman, also had business operations in Nogal and Angus. Peters had a small adobe store by the first Titsworth Store, west of the old city hall. The store also doubled as living quarters for Peters, his wife and three children. He later opened a store in the old Capitan State Bank building before the Jenkins Store in that building closed down. Peters's father built the sanitarium in Angus, and his partner's name was Andrew Lane. Lane married Gussie Rainabaugh, who married George Titsworth after Lane died.

A family named Blair had taken over the P.G. Peters store, which had moved into the Capitan State Bank building. Blair moved the store two doors down and then sold it to Joe Otero, who in turn sold it to Ben Leslie Sr.

REILY PIONEER FAMILY

In 1890, on the recommendation of his cousin George Curry, William M. Reily came to Lincoln, where he acquired the La Paloma Bar. He married Nellie Gray at Salado on October 31, 1894, and later moved to Picacho,

Hyde Shoe Shop and Barbershop about 1935 after remodeling. The barbershop was in the left side of the building, and the shoe shop was on the right. *Photograph courtesy of Garth Hyde.*

where he was postmaster. The family then moved to Roswell, where son Albert Morgan was born.

Reily next moved to Capitan and homesteaded on the north side of Magado Creek. The couple had three daughters while in Capitan: Kitty, who married Truman Spencer Sr.; Jackie, who married Will Ed Harris; and Herndon, who married Z.L. Baclawski. The original Reily ranch comprised thousands of acres north of Capitan and at one time ran three thousand head of sheep and over eight hundred head of cattle. It has been said that Seaborn Gray owned the south side of the road and William Reily owned the north side of the road.

Reily later lived in Carrizozo from 1909 until his death in March 1931. While there, his son, John Marion, and daughter, Jeanne Elizabeth, were born. Mr. Reily served as deputy sheriff, tax collector and county assessor. He was also the proprietor of the Capitan Hotel and a meat market, and he was the chair of the board of the New Mexico Institution for the Blind for over twenty years.

A TOUR OF THE VILLAGE

Herbert Lee Traylor gives a good overall description of Capitan through the years in a 1980 talk presented to the Capitan Women's Club:

> *In Capitan there were two general stores, Welch and Titsworth and P.G. Peters; these were located where the City Hall is. The Titsworth's and Peters' stores burned in 1922. Peters moved to the old adobe warehouse that Gerald Dean demolished about 1966–67. Titsworth remodeled his horse barns in the area in front of where Ruidoso State Bank now stands. The Post Office was maintained by Mrs. Larson in the two-story house across from the laundry. Bill Stewart said his mother's folks built the house in 1890. Mrs. (Ma) Julian ran a rooming and boardinghouse where Allen's Western Wear is. A fellow by the name of West ran a blacksmith shop and livery stable where the telephone company now has its utility shop. The Fishers ran a lumberyard where Kenneth Stone lives. Sam Bigger and his father printed the "Capitan Mountaineer," a weekly newspaper in a one-room house... where Lemoyne Carpenter now has his realtor's office.*
>
> *The Titsworth and Welch Co. butchered their beeves in a small house north of town by the windmill Fletcher Hall maintains just over the hill from Joiners. A fellow by the name of George Hyde had a barber and shoe*

Above: Looking south on Lincoln Avenue, circa 1920s. The school is in the center of the picture, with the Clara Larson Hotel and post office on the left. The Buena Vista Hotel and Payne's Café are on the right. *Photograph courtesy of Hollis Cummins.*

Below: Village of Capitan looking east, circa late 1930s. The "new" elementary school is in the lower left, and the Capitan Ranger Station is on the lower right. *Photograph courtesy of Historical Society of South Eastern New Mexico.*

shop in the house next or west of the Woman's Club. Gavy ran a saloon and pool hall where Carol Ramey has her shop. I've been told he also ran a laundry with the help of a Chinaman. George Titsworth lived in the house where Frances Shaw lives and Will Titsworth lived in the two-story house across the street from the bank. The two-story house on the north side of town had been moved from Coalora; later Bert Provine and family lived in it. The old bank building (Jenkin's old store) was built in 1917. A fellow by the name of White was cashier and ran it until what was known as the "Cattle Depression of 1922." It was a droughty year when all but one bank in Lincoln County failed. The Buena Vista Hotel was built in 1921–22.[33]

The railroad depot sat behind the Titsworth Store, and about six blocks south of that corner was the school. The Lincoln County Fairgrounds sit today where the school was located until it burned about 1950. In between the railroad depot and school was the Nazarene Church.[34]

The Buena Vista Hotel was another lodging establishment providing rooms for travelers visiting Capitan, and it was owned and operated by Lula Boone. Located at the corner of Lincoln Avenue and Second Street, the hotel was built in 1921 and was a drugstore before it was a hotel. At one time, it had the only neon sign in Capitan. The Buena Vista was also probably the first building wired for electricity in Capitan. Ironically, there was not electricity in the town until the 1930s. The hotel also had a dining room and

Smokey Bear Avenue looking west, circa 1950s. The third Titsworth Store is on the right side of the road. *Photograph courtesy of Hollis Cummins.*

for a time was the social mecca of Capitan, with a thriving business during the summer months. Lewis and Bessie Cummins leased the hotel from 1945 to 1947, and after their management, it was sold to Bert Cheney.

Pearl Soderback operated a restaurant named Pearl's that was the hangout for breakfast, lunch and the coffee crowds. A man named Mosier originally constructed the building as a curio shop for his wife.

An astute businesswoman, Pearl bought beef carcasses from Roswell and stored them in Cummins Store. While all of her food was good, Pearl's was known for her hamburgers and enchiladas. Burgers cost between ten and twenty-five cents, with the most popular one being the "Burger, Burger, Burger." Her enchilada plate cost one dollar and was famous as "an all day meal." She was also known for her apple pie. Pearl's standing offer to high school sports teams was, "Win the game, boys, and the ice cream is on me."[35]

Another longtime restaurant is the El Paisano, operated by several generations of the Otero family. Originally owned by Herman and Toni Otero, it is currently owned by their daughter Esther and is now operated by the third generation of that family.

After the construction of the new high school was completed in the late 1930s, a Mr. Pickering purchased the "office" of the construction crew. Pickering was the brother to Eunice Hall, whose husband Fletcher owned Sunshine Pharmacy. Pickering worked at the pharmacy prior to opening the hamburger stand. He moved the shed across the street from the high school, where he sold food to the students, sometimes on credit. When the bell rang at school letting the students out for lunch, there would be a race to see who could get to the hamburger stand first.

Pearl's Café, home of the "Burger, Burger, Burger," circa 1940s. *Photograph courtesy of Tiffany Menix.*

Capitan looking east down Smokey Bear Avenue, circa 1950s. The new high school and elementary school are at the lower right of the picture. *Photograph courtesy of Roberta Haldane.*

Mr. Pickering was also justice of the peace for Capitan. One Fourth of July, he announced there would be no fireworks in town, and anyone caught with them would answer to him. Four students took up the challenge and started down the hill west of town to gain a head of speed. They had numerous fireworks in the car with them and two lit cigars. As they drove around town they lit the fireworks and threw them out the window, causing a lot of commotion. After several passes through town, the kids parked behind the old brick school and turned off their lights, waiting to be caught and taken home to their parents. Mr. Pickering drove all around town looking for the perpetrators but never found them; eventually, the youths tired and went home. Legend has it that Pickering was told the next morning who the culprits were, and he went to their parents, but the parents refused to punish their children because they had not been caught in the act.

The main competition for George Titsworth was Murphy's Grocery Store, owned by Don Murphy and located where the library thrift store is today. The store was in the building previously occupied by Walter Lair. Murphy was connected to a wholesaler in Roswell, and during World War II, he could get things other stores could not. Don Murphy ran a good business during the 1940s and 1950s, and his son Pat took over the store when Murphy passed away.

Alvin "Blondie" Lane operated a small general store in a stone building at the corner of Fourth Street and Lincoln Avenue. Everyone who knew the

Lanes agreed on two things: Blondie was eccentric and his wife was really nice. Perhaps Blondie is best remembered for letting residents "borrow" goods from him instead of buying them.

Lane was adept at merchandising and had several stores through the years, one of which burned down. He had bought a '39 Chevy, and his wife had left him because of some dispute. Word is that he left, and when he came back, he dropped a cigarette that started the fire. He was seen sitting on a rock in front of the store laughing as the building burned down, with cans exploding on the inside.

After the first store burned down, Lane opened a second grocery store across the street in a rock building that is still standing. Blondie was reported to have been a good athlete when he was younger and actually had several banners in his store that he had won at track meets. He also had a jukebox in his store and danced when times were slow. Blondie sponsored contests for various charity fundraisers, like having students compete in a race to his store with the winners receiving a cash prize. At these events, Blondie would donate more money than the whole town put together.

Hollis Cummins tells of Blondie Lane when he was growing up:

> *Mr. Lair had a store south of the Buena Vista Motel and he hired me when I was thirteen years old paying me fifty cents a week. The Harcrow Bar was behind Lane's store and Lair went over there sometimes in the afternoon. One evening Lair caught me talking to Blondie and fired me. Blondie felt sorry for me and hired me with a raise to a dollar a week.*[36]

On a smaller scale, the Leslie and Son Meat Market serviced customers who didn't want to trade at the Titsworth Store. It was the Leslie Meat Market that took on George Titsworth in a "meat war." It is said that the Leslies won because their source of meat was cheaper: it was stolen from Titsworth's herd. The Leslies' store was extremely small. It was located just north of where village hall is today. When a customer inquired about something not currently stocked, the reply was always: "That will be on the supply truck on Monday."

George Hyde was a deaf-mute, but that did not stop him from running a combination barber and shoe shop on Lincoln Street. The barbershop was in the left front of the building and the shoe shop in the right front. In the rear of the building was the living area for the family. Hyde would cut hair on alternating days and fix shoes on the next. There were rabbits and chickens in back. Hyde was killed when he stepped out of the side of the road after cutting clover and was hit by a car.

Above: Road from Carrizozo looking east, circa 1940. *Photograph courtesy of Hollis Cummins.*

Below: George Hyde in his shoe repair store, circa 1933. *Photograph courtesy of Garth Hyde.*

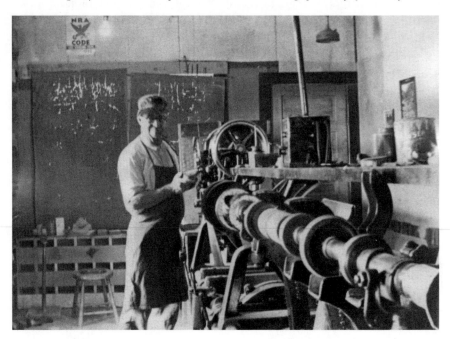

Garth Hyde grew up in Capitan and became a minister in the Nazarene Church. He spent most of his time out of state but came back repeatedly to participate in the Ranchman's Camp on Nogal Mesa. He remembers his father's store: "My dad built that structure. He built the shoe shop first

Hurt's Drug Store owned by Robert Hurt, who was later murdered near Capitan, circa 1920s. The man in the hat holding the baby is probably Robert Hurt. *Photograph courtesy of Clarence Hilburn.*

and then the living quarters in the back. When he married my mom, he doubled the size of the building and added the barbershop, which was on the side of the shoe shop. One day Dad was a barber and the next day he was a cobbler."[37]

A library was constructed prior to 1945 but later burned down. The current Capitan Library opened its doors on August 19, 1996, at the former site of Leslie and Son Meat Market on Lincoln Avenue, moving later to the old Nazarene Church building.

Hurt's Drug Store, owned by Robert Hurt, opened on Fourth Street in 1901. The villagers were entertained with a gala ball at the grand opening.[38]

The Sunshine Pharmacy, also known as Hall's Drugstore, was operated from 1921 until about 1960 by Fletcher Hall Sr. and his wife, Eunice Hall. Fletcher owned a ranch north of Capitan and later became the village's first mayor. In 1921, Hall traded his homestead for the pharmacy. There is a possibility that it was Hurt's Drug Store. The store had a soda fountain that sold milkshakes and malts and had rooms for rent upstairs.

Fletcher's son, Fletcher Jr., was born on the homestead fifteen miles north of town. He married Emma Gene Tonn, a schoolteacher, in 1945 after he returned from service during World War II. Hall operated the store until it closed in the 1960s and was active in local rodeos.

Camp Roundtree, probably the first lodging establishment in the village, was located on the northwest edge of the village near the school. There was a service station and café in front on the road and cabins in the back. The facility kept expanding until it included a cluster of trees and a motel, restaurant and service station. There was a tower with a windmill on top of the café. A pipe went from the windmill into the kitchen, where there was a storage tank.

When Roundtree died, his wife continued to operate the establishment. The site later became Hickman's Chevron Station, and the El Paisano

Above: Sunshine Pharmacy at the corner of Smokey Bear and Lincoln, circa 1950. The Larson Hotel is on the right. *Photograph courtesy of Pam Allen.*

Below: Roundtree Service Station and cabin, circa 1920s. Note the water tower in the upper left with Roundtrees written on it. *Photograph courtesy of Hollis Cummins.*

restaurant sits on the site today. The present building was built near Hall's on the other end of town and moved to this site by Wallace Ferguson.

Fisher's Lumberyard was located at Second Street and Lincoln and was operated by the widow Chloe Fisher and her son, Ben Geison. They were well respected, and people came from throughout the county to buy their lumber here. It is reported that it was a thriving business and sold good

Payne's Café and Meat Mart, circa 1920. *Photograph courtesy of the Lincoln County Historical Society.*

lumber. Mrs. Fisher owned most everything on the north side of Second Street. She is reported to have had fresh cookies for children who came into the store. Ben later became the county sheriff and county clerk.

An 1893 building that recently housed the old B&L Pizza was at one time a doctor's office and café and was first operated by the Gus Eversilt family. Around the corner, today's Chango's restaurant was built in the 1890s and at one time was a barbershop operated by "Toots" Foster. Payne's Café was previously the Central Café and was located across and down the street from the Chango building. W.B. and Lydia Payne operated the café from the 1920s to the late 1930s.

The Capitan State Bank was built on the corner of Smokey Bear and Lincoln Streets around 1910. The vault is still in the basement. Johnson Stearns relates a story about the closure of the bank in the 1920s:

> *In the period of 1923 and 1924 when livestock prices plummeted, those banks holding excessive amounts of this paper became insolvent. One of these, the Capitan State Bank, was forced to close its doors. Allie Stover, later a sheriff of this county, had sold his small place near Hondo and had taken the $900 he received to the bank in Capitan.*
>
> *Deciding he needed his money, upon arriving in Capitan he discovered the bank's plight. Bert Provine was working for the Titsworth company and*

Capitan State Bank and the second Titsworth Store, circa 1917. *Photograph courtesy of the Karol Schatzel Collection.*

Allie went there looking for what he conceived as the right answer. He asked Bert to show him some of the rifles in stock and deciding upon a 30-30 he wanted to know if Bert had a broken box of shells that he might borrow a few to try the gun out. Thus armed he proceeded across the street to the bank and sought admittance but upon being told the bank had been closed, he enforced his request with the newly acquired 30-30. Fred Pfingsten, one of the directors, being present in the bank, Allie informed him and the cashier, Mr. White, that he wanted his money back.

The two men, deciding that Allie meant what he said and appearing ready to enforce his demands with the 30-30, acquiesced and turned the funds over to him after which he proceeded to Carrizozo and placed his money in the First National Bank here.[39]

The City Garage, a General Motors dealership, was owned and operated by "Dutch" Reil. He was known to trade a car for property to bankrupt people leaving town during the Depression. The other garage in town, Liberty Garage, was a Ford dealership located across from Murphy's Store and was managed by Fred Brubaker.

Virgil "Pappy" Hall Sr. was a local resident who operated Hall's Automotive on the east end of town. Hall initially worked at the City Garage when he returned from World War II. He expanded the facility to include a Texaco service station, garage and parts store. Virgil's wife, Lydia, operated the local telephone switchboard. He became a local hero in the 1990s when the state took his driver's license away. His solution to his

Looking east down Smokey Bear Boulevard, circa 1940. The Capitan State Bank, in the center of the photograph, is now a hardware store. *Photograph courtesy of Pam Allen.*

need of transportation was to drive a John Deere tractor on the shoulder of the road. Virgil Hall Jr. took over management of the store but closed the service station and garage and currently operates only the parts store.

There were stockyards behind the old post office and the creek. Local ranchers would cut the calves from the cows and drive them to Capitan with one man in front of the calves, one on each side, and a couple behind. It was a horse race though town to get the cattle to the stockyards as dogs complicated things by chasing the cattle along the route.

Bill Nickles of Carrizozo bought the Titsworth hardware store and later sold it to Jim Black. Black managed the hardware store until his health began failing, and then he moved back to El Paso, selling the store to Gerald Dean Sr.

Gerald and Mary Dean came to Capitan from Lovington in 1959 and opened Dean Hardware Store next to Cummins' Grocery Store. Their son, Gerald Jr., married Kathy Stone in 1962, and the couple also helped with the family businesses.

Mary's brother, Virgil Wallace, and his wife, Millie, purchased the Mountain Valley Motel from Bill and Adelaide (Howard) Holmes. Wallace later added new units on the eastern end of the motel and renamed it the Smokey Bear Motel. The Beatinbow family bought the property from the

Wallaces, who continued to manage the motel for a number of years. The Beatinbows built the Smokey Bear Restaurant following the closure of Bill and Geraldine Randle's café that was located next door, where the post office is today.

NEWSPAPERS

Capitan has had at least five weekly newspapers, all published in the early twentieth century: *El Capitan, El Farol,* the *Capitan Progress,* the *Capitan News* and the *Capitan Mountaineer.*

Capitan's first newspaper was the *El Capitan,* founded in March 1900 by W.M. Clute, followed in May that same year by the *Capitan Miner,* founded by J.H. Lightfoot. The two papers merged in January 1901, becoming the *Capitan Progress* managed by Lightfoot and C.G. Nuckols. Nuckols quickly assumed control until August 1903, when all newspapers in Lincoln County merged under the Eagle Printing Company and were published as the *Capitan News,* whose motto was: "A Journal devoted to the Interests of Lincoln County." The *Capitan News* was published between August 1903 and May 1908 and was managed by J.A. Haley, who replaced Nuckols in 1905.

A Spanish newspaper, the *El Farol,* was published from December 1905 to November 1906 and later added to the interests managed by Haley. The *Capitan Mountaineer* was published by Sam Bigger and his brother Neal from

Smokey Bear Boulevard looking east, circa 1940. Sunshine Pharmacy is on the corner on the right, and the Titsworth Store is on the left. *Photograph courtesy of Pam Allen.*

May 1915 to February 1927. It was located in a building constructed in the early 1900s, across the street from the Smokey Bear Museum.[40]

Post Offices

The first post office in the area was established at Gray on August 20, 1884, with mail coming from both Roswell and San Antonio. On September 29, 1899, the first railroad car arrived at Coalora, and a three-day-a-week service was provided by a railway post office (RPO) car.[41]

On October 11, 1900, the new postmaster, Bert Rowland, changed the name of the post office to "Capitan." In December 1901, Rowland was replaced by Henry Wallace, who was then replaced by John Ritter in March 1903.

George A. Titsworth became postmaster for the first time on August 17, 1904, and held that position for almost ten years. Blosie (Mrs. Hunt) Hobbs ran the post office for Mr. Titsworth. During Titsworth's time, the post office at Richardson (Block Ranch) closed down, and mail was moved to the Capitan office. It is said that Titsworth got the mail contract under Republican administrations, and Clara Larson got the contract when the Democrats were in office.[42]

Clara Larson began her term as postmaster in April 1914. During her tenure, a star route was established to Encinoso and Deseo, with mail being delivered on alternate days. After eight years, the postmaster position reverted to George Titsworth.

The Clara Larson Hotel and post office are on the right, and the Sunshine Pharmacy is on the left, circa early 1920. *Photograph courtesy of the Lincoln County Historical Society.*

Titsworth became postmaster again on February 10, 1925, and held the position for over eight years the second time. He was followed in turn by Helen Sears, James Kent, Ann Earling, Oleta Cloud, Dixie Sparks and Frances Gardenhire Shaw.

For many years, the post office was located across the street from where the Smokey Bear Museum is located today. It was moved to the east end of the Cummins' Store location before a new post office was constructed in 1996.

One of the longtime Capitan postmasters was Frances Gardenhire Shaw. Her father, Jeff Gardenhire, brought his family to the area in 1916 and settled on the Gardenhire Half Circle Two-Bar Ranch nine miles north of Capitan. She married Jack Shaw, who came to Fort Stanton from Dexter in 1928 and worked there as an engineer for thirty-seven years. Shaw served as a village trustee in Capitan for seven years.

The Shaws' daughter, Diane, grew up in Capitan but left and was living in Roswell when she met and married Mike Riska. The couple moved back to Capitan, where Diane taught school and Mike operated a service station before retiring. Diane is currently a village counselor, and Mike operates a mail route.

Following Frances Shaw were Maxine Wright, Mike Curran and the current postmaster, Kristi Sepkowitz.

PUBLIC SCHOOLS

On April 19, 1901, Capitan was chosen as the site of the Lincoln County Teacher's Institute. The opening address was given by F.C. Matterson, who spoke about the history of education in Lincoln County. He was followed by other speakers, including county superintendent Lee H. Rudisille. The cornerstone of a two-story school was laid. Mary A. Skeham said:

> *About four years ago, the old Mexican house on the road between here and the Camp served as the school house. From there the school was transferred to a private residence...Today April 19, 1901, all these advance movements are surpassed with the laying of the corner stone of a two-story school building.*
>
> *This building will stand as a silent witness through the ages to come... Unlike the ancient times when knowledge was confined to a few, it is today becoming comparatively universal. Now the ignorant and uneducated are*

Capitan School and the women's basketball team, circa 1911. *Photograph courtesy of Hollis Cummins.*

the few: the wise and educated the many…I do invoke on this building the blessings of Heaven, and dedicate it, as far as I am able to the twin deities of Wisdom and Justice. [43]

The building, known as the Lincoln County High School, was constructed of brick and native limestone in 1901 at a cost of $13,000, raised through bonds. Harry Little did the major construction; immigrants from Mexico did the stonework. There were twelve students the first year. The school had a basketball team, but they had to wear the baseball team's uniforms. Members of the first graduating class in 1907 included Jennie Boone, Norton Spiller, William Peters, Dora Clements, Maude Bryant and Roselia Carleton.[44] By 1924, there were thirty-five students and five teachers.[45]

The school was a two-story brick building with a fire escape on the east side. Radiators were used for heating with a boiler in the basement to heat water in the pipes. Former pupils claim the building was either too hot or too cold. The students were not supposed to be on the fire escape, but almost every one of them slid down it. Behind the main building was a gymnasium.

Originally, all grades, one through twelve, were in the building, with classes combined in the limited number of classrooms. Later, when the new high school was built in 1935–36 and in operation in 1937, the fourth through sixth grades were upstairs, and first through third grades were downstairs.

By the summer of 1913, the agricultural college of Las Cruces (New Mexico State University) held a normal school for teachers in the building. Some of the county newspaper editors also referred to it as the "University Building."

Promptly at nine o'clock on Monday morning, the Normal Institute for Lincoln County was opened at the University Building by county superintendent of schools Edward J. Coe. After a short introductory address by Professor D.M. Richards of Las Cruces, the institution proceeded with classes.

Yet this was probably not the first high school in the area. The *Capitan Progress* mentions the Coalora School on several occasions. A "North School" is also mentioned, and it is unknown if these two schools are one and the same.

Seaborn T. Gray, the county superintendent of schools in 1893–94, wrote to A.H. Hudspeth: "Yes, I think about 1900 was the first public school taught by Miss Skehan in a building built by my father for the family and a part of the building was used for a school room. As I remember a part of our family and one or two Spanish children attended the school."[46]

During school year 1916–17 the class choose its first school colors, but no mention was made of the mascot. In 1924, the average daily attendance was thirty-five. Later, in 1927, the school colors of orange and black and the tiger mascot were chosen and approved by the school board.

Construction was started on a second high school in 1935 as a Works Project Administration (WPA) building. The work was completed in 1936, and the school opened in 1937. In 1945, another high school was built, and the 1936 building became a junior high school. When the new school was

Capitan Union High School, circa 1940. *Photograph courtesy of Garth Hyde.*

New Capitan Elementary School, 1950. *Photograph courtesy of Garth Hyde.*

built in 1945, there was no dressing room for the football field, so the players dressed at the old school and ran to the new school.

The original school continued to house the elementary school until it burned down in 1950. Community rumors of the time said that there was not enough funding to complete construction of the new school and the fire was set at the old school so insurance money could provide funding for the new school, but this is not correct. Although the school burned first and the gym second, the village then experienced a rash of arson in unoccupied houses around the village. A couple of boys were suspected in the crimes, but it was never proven. At that time, the elementary school was built at the current school complex by a man named McKnight.

Wally Ferguson spoke of the fire.

> *I went to school at the old grade school. When it burned down my brother Billy and Johnny Warner my cousin were the ones who sounded the alarm. They found the front doors were unlocked and open. There were a rash of buildings being burnt down in the village at that time, almost all of them were empty.*[47]

Capitan's first state athletic championship came in basketball in 1943. The Tigers football team went undefeated from 1951 to 1953 and won the state championship in 1953. There were no state playoffs in 1951 and 1952. For a small school, it has won more than its fair share of state athletic championships. The school won the state volleyball championship in 1978 and football and volleyball in 1982, as well as winning the boys track

Above: Rear of the old school showing fire damage, 1950. *Photograph courtesy of Garth Hyde.*

Below: The 1952 undefeated football team. *Front row, left to right*: Ernie Francis (30), Noah Montoya (28), unknown (29), Lloyd Cooper (14), Archie Witham (24), Melvin Romero (22), Bobby Eshom (18), Ray Keith (19), Clifton Keith (15), Tom Guck (20) and Kenny Moris (16). *Back row, left to right*: Sonny Herrera (26), Tony Archuleta (10), Charles Francis (27), Garth Hyde (25), Wally Ferguson (13), Johnny Warner (17), Dick Cox (12), Eddie Womack (11) and Lupe Otero (26). *Photograph courtesy of Eddie Womack.*

championship in 1983. This was followed by boys track in 1987, volleyball in 1988 and girls track in 1989, 1990 and 1991, with the girls' volleyball team winning the title in 2002. More recently, the boys won the state baseball title in 2011.

SCHOOL SUPERINTENDENTS

The original school superintendents were under the county school system. Capitan's first individual superintendent was C.I. Scheck, who served from 1912 to 1916. He was followed by C.V. Belknap (1916–17), C.V. Koogler (1917–18), C.F. Funk (1918), L.B. Boughman (1918–19) and D. Lambert (1919–20).

Superintendents during the 1920s and 1930s included T.P. McCallister (1920–21), W.T. Klopp (1921–23), F.S. Copeland (1923–25), Mr. Writtenburg (1925–27), D.B. Walker (1927), C.V. Koogler (1927–32), K.A. Cunningham (1932–36) and B.T. Williams (1936–43).

The 1940s to the 1960s saw R.A. Knudson (1943–44), B.T. Williams (1944–45), E.L. Hawkins (1945–47), L.W. Clark (1948–56), Bill Hall (1956–60) and D. Darling (1960–70).

Recent superintendents were Ira Caster (1970–74), R. Clifton (1975–81), David Lee (1981–83), Dr. Leonard Hayes (1983–87), L.C. Cozzens (1987–88), Scott Childress (1988–91), David Locke (1991–93), Diane Billingsley (1993–2001), Larry Miller (2001–2007) and Shirley Crawford (2007–present).

The 1939 Capitan High School basketball team. *From the left*: Coach C.C. Poling, Douglas Howell (22), Eulon Womack (88), Sam Hale (00), Hubert Burks (11), Gilbert Miranda (77), L.C. Cozzens (99), Lavario Silva (33), Wayne Cozzens (44), Grover Hightower (66), and Ben Leslie Jr. (55). *Photograph courtesy of L.C. Cozzens.*

The Cozzens family has supplied two superintendents at the Capitan schools: L.C. Cozzens and his daughter-in-law, Shirley Crawford. Seymour and Sallie Cozzens came to Lincoln County in 1924, initially living on the Nogal Mesa and then at Jacob Springs, north of Capitan, where their sons Wayne and L.C. attended school at Deseo. The family moved to Capitan and then back to the Nogal Mesa. Two daughters, Cornelia and Eileen, and another son, Doyle, were born during this time. After Seymour and Sallie moved back to Capitan, daughter Jane was born in 1940, but Sallie died in childbirth.

Cozzens went to work at the German Internment Camp at Fort Stanton in 1940 and married schoolteacher Winifred Wilkinson in 1942. The couple had two children, daughter Marilyn and son Ken. Cozzens worked around Capitan and was elected a village trustee; Winifred taught at the Capitan schools.

Wayne, L.C. and Doyle were outstanding athletes at Capitan High School, with Wayne named the greatest athlete in 1937 and 1938 and L.C. winning this award in 1939. L.C. served in the United States Marine Corps in World War II and Korea before entering the field of education. He retired in 1989 as superintendent of the Capitan schools.

Shirley Crawford is the wife of L.C. Cozzens's son, Gary, the author of this book. Originally from Roswell, and the daughter of Fletcher and Erma Crawford, Shirley became superintendent in 2007.

ENTERTAINMENT

Throughout its existence, Capitan has seen many social clubs that have since disbanded. Among them were the Territorial Theater, the Veterans of Foreign Wars, the Knights of Pythias, the Red Men's Club, the Bachelor's Club and the Kapitan Komedy Kompany. The latter was organized in North Capitan (Coalora) and performed dramas in the town hall. Organizations still in existence are the American Legion, the Capitan Women's Club and the Lions Club.

In January 1901, the Literacy Society debated the question, "Resolved that bachelors should be prohibited from Capitan?" Apparently, the vote ended in defeat for the men, as the Capitan Bachelor Club later requested that the Literary Society reconsider its verdict. The final disposition of the incident is unknown.[48]

The American Legion provides outstanding community service, including displaying flags around town on holidays, providing services at the funeral of veterans and picking up trash on the roads around the village.

During the time Fort Stanton was a military post and merchant marine hospital, there appears to have been a trail running from the fort to the nearby village of Capitan. Referred to by locals as the "Whiskey Trail," it was traveled first by soldiers and then by hospital patients seeking entertainment in Capitan.[49]

One local resident of Capitan who was present at that time stated that no one paid any attention to the official rules barring alcohol from the patients. The patients were prohibited from drinking alcohol at the fort, so they snuck out at night and used the Whiskey Trail to walk into Capitan. However, the regulations were apparently not enforced, and one bartender from Capitan actually made deliveries to the fort. There were seven bars in Capitan, with three bars alone at the end of the Whiskey Trail in the vicinity of the current Lincoln County Fairgrounds. Harcrow's Bar, owned by Alain Harcrow, and Barney's Bar, owned by Barney and Pearl Bernoski (later Soderback), were on 4th Street in Capitan, while the Buckhorn Bar was located on 5th Street. Barney's Bar moved to the east end of Highway 380, and the Buckhorn moved to 1st Street across from the present-day Smokey Bear Motel. A fourth bar, the Rusty Anchor, opened in the building that currently houses a realtor's office. It was owned first by Mr. Beauvais and then by John Annaratones. Later on, John and Pearl Soderback (the former Mrs. Bernoski) bought the Buckhorn Bar and actually made deliveries to the patients at the fort.[50]

On another occasion, Monroe Howard was reported to have been playing in an illegal poker game in the back of Herrera Bar on the south side of Second Street. Supposedly, his wife got mad at him and called the sheriff, who came and raided the poker game.[51]

Of course, patients from Fort Stanton were not the only clientele. Local cowboys from the outlying ranches also patronized these establishments.

MONROE HOWARD BAND

Beginning in the early twentieth century and continuing through the Depression era, music for local dances was provided by the Monroe Howard Band.

Howard was born in New Orleans about 1874 and moved to Texas, where he married Matilda Krueger. The couple moved to the Capitan area in 1902 and settled on a ranch south of Capitan, near the famous VV Ranch. Howard commented, "There wasn't a town of Capitan at all, just a store or two. Mr. Titsworth had a store here in 1902 and he had it quite a while before we got there."[52]

Monroe Howard Band, circa 1910. *From left to right*: Monroe Howard, James Howard and Arthur Howard. *Photograph courtesy of Nancy Hasbrouck and Donna Ikard.*

The family reports that Monroe would jab his son Jim with his fiddle bow when Jim fell asleep.[53] Monroe speaks of his time playing in the band:

> *I played the violin quite a bit when we came to Capitan. I played the violin for a living, I guess for about ten years. I had an accompanist for a while and then I finally used my two boys. One of them played the guitar [Jim] and the other the bass violin [Art]. We played this fiddling music for dances, and I played for weddings. They used to have a big hotel up at Angus. I played there and at White Oaks, Fort Stanton and Capitan. They danced most of the old-time dances—mostly squares, waltzes and two-steps. I played with Wilbur Coe when I first got here. He got to be a pretty good violinist.[54]*

BASEBALL

One of the favorite pastimes in the early twentieth century in Capitan was baseball. Villages would form teams and play one another for entertainment. Among teams in the Capitan area were those from Nogal and Fort Stanton. Monroe Howard continues:

We used to play a lot of baseball around here. I and the two Lane boys got up a team in Capitan, and Billy Ferguson, Dudge LaMay and Al Pfeiffer had a team in Nogal. Nogal was a mining town with about four hundred men, and they had a pretty good team, but we could beat the socks off of them.

Sometimes we would mix our team with the Nogal team and take on another club. It was a pretty fair amateur ball club. Billy Ferguson played shortstop most of the time. I played in the field and sometime third base. Marshall West was first base, Jody Williams pitched and Jim Crawford caught. Willie Gallacher pitched for a team we used to play against. Willie had thrown a lot of balls and was quite a ball player.

Baseball was the main sport in those days and it was a lot of fun. We used to have the games in the apple patches along the creek. Two or three hundred people would come out to watch us play. Sometimes they would get excited and rush out on the diamond, and we'd have to make them get back.[55]

RODEOS

Local rodeos began at Fort Stanton in 1900 as a way to entertain the tuberculosis patients, and they flourished until the merchant marine hospital closed in the 1950s. The rodeo was held annually for three days around the Fourth of July, with some of the patients even participating in the events. When Fort Stanton closed down, the rodeo was moved two miles east of town. The rodeos were extremely well attended, with people arriving early and staking out parking places. The Capitan/Lincoln County Rodeo had a good following until it closed down in the early 1960s, when many of its spectators started going to the new racetrack at Ruidoso Downs instead of the rodeo. Today, the rodeo is still held on the Fourth of July in conjunction with the Smokey Bear Stampede.

SMOKEY BEAR STAMPEDE

The social event of the year in Capitan is the Smokey Bear Stampede, which is held every Fourth of July weekend. It consists of a fun run, parade, rodeo and dance and is a citywide event. The colorful event is highlighted by a parade led by fire trucks, marching bands, floats and, of course, an obligatory visit from Smokey Bear. Villagers and visitors alike line both sides of the streets to observe the spectacle, while youngsters catch candy thrown from the fire trucks and floats.

LINCOLN COUNTY FAIR

The Lincoln County Fair is held annually in August at the Lincoln County Fairgrounds. The fairgrounds grew out of the Future Farmers of America (FFA)/4H. Achievement Days. The fair was begun about 1954, and the events were held at the new high school. The Lincoln County Fair Association incorporated after the gym burned. Led by Fletcher Hall Jr. and Charles and Eleanor Jones, the association raised money through the Lincoln County Roping Club, Capitan residents, local ranchers and a local philanthropist to construct the building on the fairgrounds where the original school was built. At the twentieth anniversary in 1980, the facility was named the Fletcher Hall Jr. Arena and Lincoln County Community Center in recognition of Mr. Hall's dedication to the fair and rodeo.[56]

HORSE RACING

For a while into the early twentieth century, Capitan was a magnet for horse racing and, as early as 1903, had a formal racetrack.[57] Monroe Howard describes that sport:

> *We did quite a bit of horse racing when I first came to this part of the country. Not big races. Sometimes there would be three or four horses in sweepstake races, and sometimes there would be just two-horse matches. Some of the horses were regular racehorses. I brought two here, one named Steamboat. He got that name because of his big feet, but he was pretty fast. They would have meetings and advertise them.*[58]

No local horse garnered more attention than Steamboat, which was born one April afternoon in 1907 on Nettie Peebles's Little Creek Farm. He was deep brown in color, with a white spot on his forehead and deep black hair on his mane and tail and long hair on his fetlocks. His one exception was that he was significantly larger than the other colts in the region. Local cowboys referred to him as "the big colt."

The colt quickly grew to fifteen hands and 1,300 pounds in two years. About the same time, the colt began making advances on the fillies and found himself in the gelding pasture. The proprietor of a local sawmill, a man named Clyde Humphrey, bought the horse and turned to his cowboys and asked, "Do you think you can lead that Steamboat home?" The colt had its name.

In his third year, Steamboat worked in the forest pulling a wagon. He soon began to spook easily and repeatedly ran off with the wagon still attached. The mill owner tried pairing him with a mule named Jude in an attempt to cease Steamboat's bolting ways.

The owner, reportedly a man named Will Stack, soon agreed that Steamboat needed to participate in the local horse races. Steamboat was broken to ride and was outrunning local horses with little effort. At this time, he weighted 1,450 pounds and wore a number four shoe, running a quarter mile in twenty-four seconds. In a short time, Steamboat had mastered most of the local horses and then was taken to Texas, where he ran successful races. There was no money to support a full-time rider and trainer, so the horse was brought back to Capitan.

The whole area was enthralled with sweepstake races. Will Slack's horse, Black Tom, won the race in 1912. The following year, an entertainment day was organized for July 17, 1913, with a sweepstake race as the opening event. Entered in the 1913 race were Seaborn Gray's mare, John W. Owen's mare, Marshall West's mare and a pony from the Mescalero Reservation. The horses finished the race in that order.[59]

Seaborn Gray had a black horse named Capitan that was beating other horses in the area. Another mare named Tijuana Mare was brought up to Capitan to race against the horse Capitan. As soon as Steamboat's owners became aware of this, they entered Steamboat in the race.

The race took place at Fort Stanton during the Fourth of July activities in 1914 and drew a crowd. No count was taken that day, but everyone agreed that every prominent citizen in the area was in attendance, including the governor, William C. McDonald. According to local legend, the three judges for the race were Monroe Howard, J.H. McMillan and Marshall West. Arch Parker was the starter.

Lots were drawn for the starting position, with Tijuana Mare on the inside position to the left, Capitan in the middle and Steamboat on the right. When the horses were brought to the line, Steamboat stood motionless while the other two horses were restless. Finally, the starter decided it was as fair a lineup as possible and started the race.

Legend says that when the starting gun went off, Steamboat jumped straight up in the air, and the three horses were off, neck and neck until the last few yards of the race, when Steamboat pulled ahead and won by a good length. Capitan beat Tijuana Mare by a neck.

Many years after the famous race, Herbert Lee Traylor was attending a picnic at Hondo that included horse races with animals from Roswell,

Corona, Capitan and Tinnie. Steamboat was nowhere to be seen, but when the races were over, a horse from Roswell had won by a close margin. A little while later, a man approached the owner of the Roswell horse and asked if he would like to run his horse with one from the White Mountains. A group of men went around the corner of the grounds, where a team of draft horses was tied to a wagon and a man was sitting on a lard can. The man was asked if he would race his horse against the horse from Roswell. According to Traylor, the man responded, "Yes, I'll race Steamboat if there is something involved other than pocket change."

The time for the race was set for 3:00 p.m., and at that time, two riders from Roswell brought their horses to the starting line and chose their positions. They were soon joined by the man sitting on the lard can, who brought Steamboat to the starting line using homemade racing tack. Supposedly, bets were made freely that day, and a liberal amount of money was wagered.

Though normally very calm at the start of a race, this day Steamboat was nervous and jumped at the starting line. Finally, it was decided there was a fair start, and the horses were off. Steamboat took the early lead, and after a couple hundred yards, his rider was standing up and waving to the other horses to come and join him. Observers reported that the ground shook like an earthquake when Steamboat ran by. He won by a wide margin in what was his last race. Steamboat was sold to a forest ranger, and it was reported that the ranger's grandchildren rode him in the years prior to World War II.[60]

Every Friday for a time, the local Hispanics had a "gallo pulling." They would bury a rooster with just its neck sticking out of the ground. The cowboys would ride by as fast as they could and lean over and try to grab the rooster by the neck and pull it out of the ground. This practice has long since been discontinued.

Religion

Spiritual life in Capitan has been provided by several denominations over the years. Religions represented include the Capitan Community Fellowship, the Church of Christ, the Methodist Church, the Baptist Church, the Four Square Church and the Sacred Heart Catholic Church, which is probably the oldest church in the village.

One of the first references to religious activities was noted in 1900 when a Sunday school was organized in North Capitan.

The Ranchman's Camp is located about eight miles west of Capitan. Founded in 1940, this non-denomination revival focuses on the cowboys in

Capitan Methodist Church in 1948. *Photograph courtesy of Garth Hyde.*

Lincoln County. The Ranchman's Camp, still an annual event, is served by itinerant preachers.

At one time, there was literally a church on almost every street corner. At the corner of Third and White Oaks, there were the Methodist, Catholic and Baptist churches. The Jehovah's Witness Kingdom Hall was across the street from the Titsworth Store and looked like a garage.

The Nazarene Church, founded west of town in 1916, moved into Capitan and held services in various buildings until a permanent church was built in 1921. After serving its members in Capitan for many years, the church moved to Angus in 1976.

MILITARY SERVICE

Capitan has sent its sons and daughters to fight the nation's wars since it was founded in 1900. Even before the village was established, many of the local men, particularly from Fort Stanton, had served in the Civil War and the Indian Wars. Some cowboys, including future governor George Curry, from local ranches served in the Rough Riders during the Spanish-American War.

Young men from Capitan, along with many who were to move there in later years, served in World War I. Twenty-three men from Lincoln County perished during World War I, including George A. Chavez of Capitan, who died of influenza.

World War II saw a significant contribution of service by a high percentage of Capitan men. Unfortunately, that high percentage also meant many deaths among these men serving their country.

Like many other communities across the United States during the Depression, several young men joined the National Guard. With the coming of World War II, the New Mexico National Guard's 200th Coast Artillery was activated and placed in national service. Initially training at Fort Bliss in El Paso, Texas, the 200th Coast Artillery was posted to the Philippines when the war started.

For the first three months of the war, the New Mexicans fought on the Luzon Peninsula before surrendering with the remainder of American forces on April 9, 1942. After the surrender, the New Mexicans were among the American units that made the brutal sixty-five-mile Baatan Death March from Mariveles to the prisoner of war camps at San Fernando. Upon reaching San Fernando, the men were put on railroad cars and sent to Camp O'Donnell. Kemp Pepper died while a prisoner of war (POW) after the Bataan Death March. Camp O'Donnell was where hundreds died from disease and starvation, or they died when they lost the will to live. It has been estimated that one in six Americans died during the first six weeks at Camp O'Donnell. John Norton, of Capitan, also died at Camp O'Donnell on June 11, 1942.

Later in the war, the Japanese started moving the prisoners to Japan and China by ship. On October 24, 1944, the *Arisan Maru* was sunk and over one hundred New Mexicans were lost, among them Mervin J. Williams of Capitan. The *Oryuko Maru* was sunk by American airplanes on December 15, with a loss of three hundred Americans, including Benjamin Leslie of Capitan.

With the end of the war, POW camps in Japan were liberated. One of those men liberated at Osaka was James Patterson of Capitan.

Those men from Capitan who lost their life but were not captured in the Philippine Islands include Robert Bigger, who drowned in Louisiana; Robert Luck, who died in the liberation of the Philippines in 1945; and Walter Robinson, who was killed in Italy in 1944 and later awarded the Distinguished Service Cross, the second-highest award in the army, second only to the Congressional Medal of Honor.

Louis Otero lost his life in the Korean War after being taken as a prisoner of war in November 1950. He died in captivity on March 30, 1951. Though not killed, Margarito "Maggie" Trujillo was captured and spent several years in a North Korean prisoner of war camp before being repatriated and returned to the United States.

Navy Quartermaster Second Class Chester Dale was killed in Vietnam on November 1, 1968, by an explosive device at Go Cong.

Located in downtown Capitan at the corner of U.S. Highway 380 and State Road 246 is the Capitan Veterans' Memorial. On the memorial are two plaques. The first reads: "Monument Designed by Epifanio Carvajal and Boney Zamora (circa 1950)." The second one reads: "In Memory of All Those Who Served Their County During Peace and Wartime. (American Legion Post #57)."

CHAPTER 3

"MOTHER" JULIAN

Every so often, a special person comes into a community, and in Capitan, this special person was Anna "Mother" Julian. Though named Anna, she was known locally as "Mother Julian" or just "Ma Julian." Born on December 12, 1864, in Montgomery County, Arkansas, Anna Ritchey married James B. Julian in 1887 in Benton, Arkansas. The couple moved to Coalora in April 1901. There are rumors that James abused alcohol during the marriage. Local legend has it that James Julian went out one day, harnessed his team to his wagon and drove off, never to be seen again. One story has him landing in Los Angles and becoming a successful businessman active in local politics. Mother Julian divorced him in 1921, long after he deserted her.[61]

Mother Julian later married Samuel Wells of White Oaks, but that marriage ended in divorce in 1930, when she was about sixty-six.[62] Samuel Wells would borrow all of Anna's cash, as well as that of friends, load up his burro with food and whiskey and disappear to find a gold mine.

Wells would go several miles from town and camp until his supplies ran out, and then he would come home with samples of ore he had found. From the samples he brought in, he was able to finance more supplies and go out again. When he had no more supplies or ore, he would go back to Mother Julian's hotel and play poker at the kitchen table or roost on a wooden box behind the stove and watch his wife do all of the work. Mother Julian describes her husband:

> *I had a full house as it was Christmas Day, every room taken, and I had*
> *to set the table three times in order to feed them all. At the last table were a*

Anna "Mother" Julian. *Photograph courtesy of Roberta Haldane.*

Aerial view of Capitan taken circa 1940s. The elementary school is in the lower left of the picture. The ranger station is in upper left, and the new high school is in the upper center. *Photograph courtesy of Hollis Cummins.*

lot of high-toned people, tourists I guess, who although nice enough, seemed a little fussy and I did not want anything to happen to spoil their dinner.

My old man had been drinking all the morning, mostly the free Tom and Jerry's the saloons were furnishing, and when he came back to the hotel he was whiskey mean.

I closed the door from the kitchen into the dining room, and slammed him down on the wood box behind the stove, and told him to sit there and shut up. Then he begged me for ten dollars, again I told him to shut up. Then he threatened if I didn't give him the money he would beat me, but I grabbed the ax and he sat down and kept quiet. Every time I'd pass him he'd whisper, "Mother, give me ten dollars or I'll beat you." As there was a dance on that night all the ranch people had left their babies with me to look after. I was on the jump, waiting on the table, and keeping the twenty odd babies quiet.

For dessert I had served the first and second tables three kind of pie, but for the tourists I had in the oven a big egg custard. It was in a big pan

61

and held some two gallons. I came down stairs from tending the babies, and had taken away the empty plates, telling the folks I would bring in their desert. After they had all been served I started to the kitchen with the container which was still about half full of sticky egg custard. As I entered the kitchen and closed the door behind me, there stood Wells with a big stick of wood in his hand. "Give me that ten dollars, you hear me? I want it right now." Down I came on his head with that big pan, custard and all, and crumpled him flat…the last I heard of him he had taken his burros and left for the hills; anyway, I divorced him and took back my first husband's name. [63]

Roberta Haldane paints a picture of Mother Julian:

A colorful figure straight out of a Norman Rockwell painting, rail thin and stooped, she was over eighty years of age…to me as a child of nine or ten she looked older than God. She wore a long calico print dress that almost touched the ground, an apron over the dress, old-fashioned black shoes, and a sunbonnet of the sort that ties under the chin and has a stiffened brim jutting out over the face.

To me she looked like a gypsy, with her dark skin and piercing, almost black eyes. She asked Grandmother if I could walk back with her to her house to show me her "place," which she seemed very proud of. I was fascinated by the many little sculptured animals she had all around… squirrels, birds, rabbits, etc. When it was time to leave, she asked me to choose one of her animals to take home. I cherished my "chalk" bunny for years. Obviously, Mother Julian was a kind woman who liked children. I seem to recall that she never had children of her own. [64]

Anna Julian moved her business from Coalora to Capitan in 1905. Setting up her boardinghouse, which was simply known as "Mother Julian's," on Lincoln Street where the Capitan Village Hall sits today, Mother Julian embarked on a legendary journey. Her establishment was a two-story frame building with a long porch in front holding chairs for the lodgers to use following a hearty meal. Downstairs, adjacent to the kitchen, was a large room containing a long table with ample chairs to seat the guests. There were five or six rooms upstairs for patrons who aimed to stay all night.

The main boarders at Mother Julian's were cowboys from the various ranches in the area. Cowboys from the Block Ranch stayed at her boardinghouse whenever they were in Capitan. Ed Downing came to town

Road coming east from Lincoln. The Titsworth Store is the large building to left of the Salado Creek, and the old school is to the left of the picture. *Photograph courtesy of Hollis Cummins.*

once a week with a four-horse wagon to pick up supplies at the Titsworth Store. He would come to town, load his wagon at the store, spend the night at Mother Julian's and then return to the ranch the following day.

Another boarder who stayed at Mother Julian's when he was in town was Judge Andrew H. Hudspeth. Judge Hudspeth, of Carrizozo, who later became a New Mexico Supreme Court justice, is remembered as presiding over the trial of Bessie Hurt, who tried to shoot George Titsworth after the second murder trial of her father's accused killers.[65]

One time, Mother Julian told local cowboy Newt Kemp that she wanted to ride his horse. Newt told her okay but admonished her to "keep the forked end down."[66]

One of the main reasons for Mother Julian's success was that she understood the appetites of men. She served miners, cowboys and Texans. Anna Julian succeeded in her boardinghouse because she catered to their needs and served what her tenants wanted. Her meals were pure and simple. John Sinclair wrote:

> *Dinner at noon would feature a huge pot of pinto beans boiled down with heavily salted pork. There might be Texas meats like narrow-guts or sweetbreads, steaks fried very well-done with milk gravy, a platter holding a five-inch mound of fried potatoes, and bowls of rice, that great range-country comestible cooked in various styles. Mother Julian baked a tasty rice pudding, heavily seasoned with nutmeg and cinnamon, rich with raisins, milk and butter. It was cowboy food alright, but mighty different from what batching riders mixed for themselves out on range camps, mere rice and raisons and sugar boiled in water.[67]*

She was also known for her breakfasts of homemade biscuits with fresh local eggs and thick bacon, with a side of fried potatoes. There were many brands of coffee, but Mother Julian always served Arbuckles, known as "the coffee that made the West." Other meals might consist of oysters and pork, but never mutton because most of her diners were Texans, and they would say, "Wool gets gummed up in my teeth."[68]

The proprietor of each boardinghouse had his or her own rules, with one featured in particular, and Mother Julian was no exception. With Mother Julian catering to cowboys, there was a large dishpan sitting on a stand by the kitchen door called a "wreck pan." Having finished his meal, each diner was expected to pick up his dinner wreck (plate and utensils) and place it in the wreck pan. This was a rule adhered to by cowboys out on the range and enforced by Mother Julian in her establishment.[69]

At night, after all the evening dishes were cleared, those present would sit around the table. Soon someone would persuade Mother Julian to speak of her reminiscences, which were rumored to sometimes last all night. Mrs. Pons eventually bought the boardinghouse and changed the name to Pons Boarding House.

Mother Julian passed away on Saturday, June 28, 1952. Services were held the following Sunday, and she was buried in the Capitan Cemetery. Her tombstone reads: "Love Light My Way to God."[70]

CHAPTER 4
THE TITSWORTH EMPIRE

B orn in Indiana in 1867, George Titsworth was a man of short stature and pleasant disposition. He moved to Colorado at age eighteen and went to work in the general merchandising business. Sometime before November 1901, George moved to Capitan and purchased one-half interest in the E.B. Welch hardware and grocery business. He began his tenure in the grocery business by delivering groceries in a wheelbarrow.

By 1905, George had acquired enough resources to build the most substantial two-story house in downtown Capitan. The roomy house, built by Frank English of Carrizozo, is still in use today.

Sometime in the early 1900s, at nearby Bonito, George met and befriended newlyweds Andrew Lane and his wife, Gussie Rainabaugh Lane, an attractive woman born in 1877. The Lanes, who had moved to the Bonito area for health reasons, moved again before too long to Socorro, where Andrew passed away. Gussie then returned to her home in Maryland with her five-year-old son, also named George.

George Titsworth began writing to Gussie after her return to Maryland, and a courtship through the mail culminated in the couple's marriage in Socorro in 1908. Returning to Capitan, the couple lived there until George died in October 1949, and Gussie followed him in 1970. Both are buried in the Capitan Cemetery. They were survived by sons Allen and George A. Jr.; a daughter, Elizabeth Titsworth Wilson; and Gussie's son, George Andrew Lane.

Will Titsworth, George's brother, came to Lincoln County before 1910 and married Annie Coe. He became a major participant in the Titsworth

Above: Original Welch and Titsworth Store, circa 1905. George A. Titsworth is standing in the doorway. *Photograph courtesy of Hollis Cummins.*

Below: The George A. Titsworth house in 1908. *From left to right*: Elizabeth Furman Rainabaugh, Gussie Irene Rainabaugh, George Andrew Lane and George A. Titsworth. *Photograph from Margie Titsworth Slayton Estate collection.*

Store activities before passing away in Roswell on February 3, 1938, and he was buried at Glencoe. A third brother, Fred, came to Capitan in 1921, reportedly to be the bodyguard for George. Fred's son, Frank, married Mora Ferguson in 1931 and operated several businesses in the Hondo Valley.

Third Titsworth Company Store looking west along Smokey Bear Boulevard, circa 1925. *Photograph from Margie Titsworth Slayton Estate collection.*

About 1912, the brothers bought a ranch in the Tinnie area from Pedro Analla that had extensive apple orchards, and the Titsworths soon built an apple-packing plant. In the eastern end of the plant was a room for cleaning and packing apples; the western end served as storage for filled apple crates before they were loaded on trucks at the loading dock and trucked to Capitan. At Capitan, the crates were stacked onto railroad cars and shipped throughout the state. The brothers also raised sheep at the Tinnie Ranch.

Will expanded his own business by purchasing the Sunset Ranch, located in the Hondo Valley, in 1913, renaming it the Hondo Valley Fruit Company, which produced apples, lettuce, cabbage and alfalfa for shipment to Capitan. The brothers added horses, cows and pigs. George Coe, a Lincoln County pioneer, wrote in 1956 that the Titsworths did a "tremendous business" and "supplied the majority of ranchers and farmers and county stores in all of Lincoln County. He sold everything from a hairpin to a threshing machine."[71]

When the brothers arrived at Capitan, the village had around three hundred people, and the El Paso and Northeastern (later South Pacific) railroad line had been laid in 1899. George soon realized he could use the rail line to import goods the twenty-one miles up the mountain from Carrizozo to Capitan.

The Titsworths' holdings did not end with the grocery, dry goods and hardware business. George owned the well used by the village and railroad, and he also owned a car dealership and gas station. For a steady paycheck,

Remodeled Titsworth Company Store, circa 1910. Note that Titsworth had bought out Welch by this time. *Photograph courtesy of Hollis Cummins.*

he served as postmaster of Capitan from August 17, 1904, to April 18, 1920, and again from February 10, 1929, to October 9, 1933.

The village of Capitan was growing and prospering. Eventually buying out E.B. Welch, George Titsworth located his original store at the northeast corner of Smokey Bear Boulevard and Lincoln Avenue. Soon after, he added more groceries and hardware and ventured into the wholesale business, where he sold his wares, some say at inflated prices and high interest credits, to locals.

The first store burned about 1911 and was soon rebuilt on the same location. The second Titsworth Store, also located on the northeast corner of Smokey Bear and Lincoln, burned on October 17, 1923, with a loss of over $100,000 in merchandise. [72] However, store operations continued in the company's warehouse until a new store could be built, utilizing the barn as the new store. The final Titsworth Store was built next to the curb of Smokey Bear Street/Highway 380 in about 1924. Tragedy again struck in 1929 when Salado Creek overflowed and carried most of the foodstuffs to the flats below Capitan. Titsworth drove his team down to the flats to salvage any goods that could be saved. The Titsworth Company also butchered its own beef in a small house north of the village.

By 1905, the Coalora coalfields had played out, and the El Paso and Northeastern tried to tear up the spur line between Carrizozo and Capitan. Titsworth was successfully able to convince the railroad to keep the spur line

Second Titsworth Company Store, circa 1912. *Photograph from Margie Titsworth Slayton Estate collection.*

open, citing the need to supply Fort Stanton. In the process, the railroad depot in Coalora was moved to Capitan in 1906.

About the same time, the Titsworths won several lucrative contracts with the Fort Stanton Merchant Marine Hospital A partial list of items sold by Welch and Titsworth to Fort Stanton for February 1907 includes 250 pounds of beans, 1,625 pounds of bran, 862 pounds of butter, 24 pounds of chocolate, 6 quarts each of lemon extract and vanilla extract, 1,575¾ dozen eggs, 7 barrels of flour, 50 pounds of walnuts, 6,473 pounds of Irish potatoes, 600 pounds of table salt, 1,900 pounds of sugar, 8,891 pounds of beef carcasses, 18 pounds of horseshoe nails and 55 gallons of kerosene.

In the month of July 1909 alone, Titsworth did $9,467.47 business with the hospital. Also during that year, he sold $8,000.00 in coal to the Hospital at $7.50 per ton. Titsworth was able to provide these materials because he bought them in bulk from as far away as Las Vegas, Socorro and El Paso and shipped them via the railroad to Capitan.

The Titsworth horse corral was located just south of where the fairgrounds are today. Titsworth sold a lot of horses to Fort Stanton, and when a shipment arrived, Titsworth's cowboys drove them right through town to the horse pens.

While the Fort Stanton hospital was an excellent source of income, George did not limit his business to government contracts. He also served the villages of Capitan, Lincoln and Coalora, as well as the local ranches and homesteads.

George A. Titsworth, circa 1930s. *Photograph courtesy of the Karol Schatzel Collection.*

It was during World War I that Titsworth's empire began to expand and take shape. Along with his brother Will, George formed a corporation and acquired parcels of land on debts until the Titsworth Corporation became a business force to be reckoned with.

A bank was located within the Titsworth Mercantile building with a teller housed in a cage. In 1929, when the Great Depression hit, there was a run on banks, and all banks, including the one in the Titsworth Store, did not pay out accounts to patrons. George Hyde went across the street from his shoe store and wrote a note to the teller requesting to withdraw the money from his account. The teller told him that no one was allowed to withdraw his money. Hyde went home, came back with a paper bag and handed the clerk the same note requesting the money, but this time when the clerk looked up, he was staring at a pistol being held by George Hyde. The clerk went to get George Titsworth, who came back to talk to Hyde. In the background, Pat Dixon was heard to say, "What ya gonna do now, Mr. Titsworth?" Titsworth replied, "I am going to give him his money," and he did.[73]

In January 1943, the Titsworth warehouse, located behind the store, burned to the ground with a total loss of its contents reported at over $25,000. While the store was threatened by the fire, a heroic effort by the Capitan Volunteer Fire Department saved it from destruction.

L.C. Cozzens worked for the Titsworth Company when he was attending Capitan High School in the 1930s:

Above: George A. Titsworth in his office, circa 1940. *Photograph courtesy of the Karol Schatzel Collection.*

Below: Railroad cars being unloaded onto Titsworth Company trucks, circa 1915. *Photograph from Margie Titsworth Slayton Estate collection.*

I was a gopher—I did whatever they told me to do. When I got older, my brother Wayne and I drove a delivery truck in Capitan, and later I inherited the delivery routes in the local area. It was a supply route for the stores in the county. A guy named Orland Wilson [who married Titsworth daughter Elizabeth] *would go around on Monday and take orders.*

They would stage the orders during the week and I would deliver them on Friday. The railroad cars were loaded with supplies and unloaded right at the depot into the Titsworth warehouse. The warehouse was north of the depot and there was a ramp from the trail to the warehouse. The corrals were at the end of the track on the north side.[74]

RUSHER INCIDENT

In July 1905, Jesse "Fate" Avant of the New Mexico Mounted Police, took custody of Robert Rusher, also known as "Russie," and charged him with burning down a house in Capitan. Avant also suspected Rusher and others of stealing horses. He escorted Rusher to jail in Lincoln on July 18. Sometime later that evening, Rusher escaped.[75]

The following morning, Deputy Sheriff Phil Blanchard was in Capitan looking for Rusher, with the *Capitan News* describing Rusher's escape as "left jail, without hobbles, or bell, and without any instructions to the sheriff about forwarding his mail."[76] While Blanchard was unable to locate Rusher, it was believed that he remained in the area.

During the first week of August, Avant reported to his supervisor that the cattle rustling business in Capitan had shown a marked decline and that suspected rustlers were leaving town. This was followed on August 19 with a report by Avant to Captain John Fullerton describing his stakeout in the Welch and Titsworth Store and pre-dawn patrols aimed at apprehending the remaining local rustlers.[77] It seems a prisoner in the jail in Lincoln was allowed to escape and rob the Capitan store. A local rancher captured the escapee and returned him to the jail.[78]

On Tuesday, August 22, Avant's son, Bundy, rushed into the Avants' home to inform his father that that he had found a cow from the Angus VV Ranch tied up in his north pasture. About sundown, Avant was hiding in the bushes when three rustlers rode up and killed the cow and started to skin it. About the time a fourth rustler showed up, Avant jumped up from his hiding place and told the rustlers to surrender. One complied, but the other three jumped into the underbrush and returned fire. The firefight lasted until the rustlers ran out of ammunition. Avant arrested Abran Miller and Severo Perez and took them before Judge J.A. Haley, who placed them in jail with a fifty-dollar bond each. The carcass of the cow was returned to the VV Ranch.[79]

Bundy Avant was with his father that day and remembers the event this way: "Father raised up from our hiding place and told the [four] men to

Interior of the Titsworth Company Store, circa 1908. *Photograph courtesy of the Karol Schatzel Collection.*

put their hands up, that they were under arrest. The bullets went flying ,but as we had the protection of the canyon bank, the men soon saw it was the better [part] of valor to surrender."[80]

Two days after the rustlers' arrest, Avant learned from one of Capitan's "working girls" that one of her customers was going to rob the Welch and Titsworth Store that evening. Avant informed George Titsworth, and for a second time in recent days, the two men staked out the store after it closed that evening.

Avant and Titsworth hid in the store, and when the burglar broke in through a side window, he was ordered by Avant to throw up his hands. The burglar, who turned out to be Robert Rusher, emptied the six-shooter he was carrying into the darkness but hit neither Titsworth nor Avant. They returned fire and hit Rusher with buckshot, killing him.[81]

The coroner's inquest noted that both Avant and Titsworth returned fire after Rusher was told to surrender. It was not determined which man fired the fatal shot, but an article in the *Las Vegas Daily Optic* identified Avant as firing a shotgun. Rusher died near the front door, continuing to fire his pistol as he fell.

The local newspapers told the story in this manner:

Buckshot, as well as pistol balls were soon flying thick and fast. Ten buckshot took effect on Rusher's body, and he fell near the front of the store, and his body was found face downward, a 32-calibre pistol grasped in his right hand, all six chambers of the chambers empty.[82]

The next morning, a coroner's jury found five finger rings and four pocket watches bearing the Welch and Titsworth trademark in Rusher's pocket. The jury ruled that Rusher's death "was justifiable homicide, and that the deceased met his death while resisting lawful arrest."[83]

HOMESTEADS

The Enlarged Homestead Act of 1909 doubled the amount of land available to a homesteader from 160 acres to 320 acres. This did not seem to be controversial on the surface, but all of the prime land in Lincoln County had been settled and what remained were the more remote areas with little or no water. The land was marginal at best, but settlers still tried to farm it.

In 1916, Congress passed the Stock Raising Homestead Act on the heels of the Enlarged Homestead Act, raising the allocation to 640 acres, or one square mile. It is here that the controversy swirling around George A. Titsworth resides.

For established merchants like the Titsworths, it was relatively easy to expand their landholdings through loans and extending credit to locals who were homesteading the poor land. When the loan or bill became due, such as when a crop was harvested, the settler was expected to pay off the loan or the land would be collected as collateral.

When George Titsworth was implicated in the murder of a local pharmacist, Robert Hurt, a public opinion letter appeared in a local newspaper describing the situation:

Capitan and the surrounding vicinity is a small community. Geo. A. Titsworth, the head of the Titsworth Company, went to that community thirty years ago, a poor man. He is a modest man and of but few words, but he is a man of unusual business judgment. By his frugality, industry, and tact, he has built up prosperous business as a merchant and ranchman. He has acquired a number of stock ranches and orchard lands from which he has derived large profits, and conducts the largest wholesale and retail store in the county. He has been for

The third Titsworth Company Store, circa 1925. *Photograph courtesy of Hollis Cummins.*

many years, and is now, the dependence of the people around him for their family supplies. He has at all times been kind to them—gave them credit, and trusted them when they needed help. He is liberal in responding to all kinds of charitable demands. More than anyone else in his neighborhood, he has been a benefactor to the community in which he resides, and yet this man, who has meant so much to those whom he has helped, has been published far and wide as the man who inspired the death of a neighbor.[84]

THE HURT MURDER

Local lore alleges that in one incident, local pharmacist and rancher Robert Hurt had upset George Titsworth, who in turn allegedly arranged for Hurt to have a "hunting accident." Robert Hurt was a wealthy pharmacist and rancher who owned a ranch northeast of Capitan. He was murdered on the evening of January 24, 1923. Hurt had bought supplies in Capitan and was shot nine times with a 30-30 rifle and a shotgun as he crossed a dry arroyo two miles east of town in a light wagon. Physical evidence indicated that two men were hiding in the bushes on the west side of the arroyo.[85]

Robert A. Hurt was born in Grayson County, Texas, on December 29, 1871. He attended Buffalo Gap College and the University of Texas

Photograph of Hurt family, circa 1906. Robert Hurt, Katie Hurt (center) and Myrtle Meers Hurt. *Photograph courtesy of Clarence Hilburn.*

Pharmacy Department. Coming to Capitan in 1899, he married Myrtle Meers on November 10, 1902. He was a rancher with cattle and sheep, a justice of the peace and the county assessor, in addition to managing his pharmacy in Capitan.[86]

Titsworth and Hurt had certainly been feuding for a time. Someone, possibly Hurt, had reported the Titsworth Company for illegally dispensing prescription drugs in 1921.[87] While impossible to verify, another local rumor held Hurt responsible for the Titsworth Store's burning down and, at different times, for torching hayfields east of town and stealing cattle in the early 1920s.

District attorney J. Benson Newell conducted the investigation into the murder. When the first shot was fired, Hurt jumped from the wagon and tried to get behind a galvanized tank on the bed of the wagon. There were bullet holes in both the bed of the wagon and the tank. It was alleged that on the day of the murder, Hunter "Hunt" Hobbs borrowed a rifle and pair of overshoes from Tom Simer. The day after the murder, tracks corresponding to those at the murder site were found at the Titsworth Store, and a 30-30 rifle was found inside.

They (the bushwhackers) were hidden under the rocks up there in that little old grove. They were shooting at Hurt and he got down by the horses and started walking. They saw where he was walking by the side of that team. They killed one of the horses and killed old Bob Hurt. Then they got out of there and Will Titsworth got stuck in the road down there. He went down there to see about it. I guess you heard the old story. Dad said they had some shoes, and put 'em in the stove but they didn't set them on fire.[88]

In February 1923, Hunt Hobbs and Tom Simer were arrested by Sheriff Harris and charged with the murder of Hurt. Will Titsworth was charged as an accomplice. All three of the accused had close ties to George Titsworth: Will Titsworth managed the farming operation in the Hondo Valley; Hunt Hobbs was ranch foreman for George Titsworth; and Tom Simer worked for Titsworth and had a substantial house north of Capitan.

Jess Stansill, an El Paso detective, testified that a man driving a team in the arroyo could not have seen a person hiding in the brush above the bank. A soft-nosed 30-30 bullet was found in Hurt's body, and 30-30 shells were found on the bank. Overshoes found in Tom Simer's house in Capitan fit the tracks at the murder site perfectly. Governor James Hinkle lent bloodhounds from the state penitentiary, and they tracked to Simer's house, where the overshoes were found.

The initial hearing was held on February 19, 1923, in Carrizozo. Carrizozo was bristling with armed men, and feelings ran strong for both sides. Judge Edwin Mechem, of the Third Judicial District, presided over the trial. The state was represented by J. Benson Newell, district attorney of the Third Judicial District; George W. Prichard, of White Oaks, represented the defendants.[89]

At the hearing, Mrs. Arthur Rogers of Fort Stanton testified that she heard Will Titsworth tell Hurt, "I'll get you," in an argument with Hurt earlier in the day. L.H. Merrill testified that he saw Will, Hunt Hobbs and Tom Simer in an automobile between Capitan and the scene of the crime on the day of the murder, and later that day, he saw Will alone in the car heading back to Capitan. The defense did not present a case at the hearing, and Judge Edwin Mechem bound over the defendants with a bond of $15,000 each. Former state senator and cattleman J.V. Tully of Ruidoso posted the bonds.[90]

The trial was moved to Alamogordo in an attempt to get a fair jury. Judge Edwin Mechem again presided. Held on February 3, 1924, the trial ended with a hung jury. A second trial was also held in Alamogordo, with Judge Raymond Ryan presiding. District Attorney Newell again represented the

The third Titsworth Company Store, circa 1930s. Hunt Hobbs is on the horse to the right, and George Titsworth is under the porch wearing a white shirt and tie. *Photograph courtesy of the Karol Schatzel Collection.*

state, but this time the defense team consisted of Hiram Dow, Louis Fullen, George Prichard, A.H. Hudspeth and J.S. Vaught.

The prosecution introduced no new evidence. However, the defense introduced a ballistics specialist, who said that neither the shell casings nor the bullets taken from Hurt's body matched the rifle found at the Titsworth Store. The defense next successfully challenged the credibility of the bloodhound expert and found that the dogs were put on a cold trail over a week old and that the "expert," was, in fact, a convicted felon. Finally, a large number of prominent Lincoln County citizens testified as to the character of the defendants. A verdict of not guilty was returned.[91]

After the second trial, Hurt's fifteen-year-old daughter, Bessie Hurt, confronted George Titsworth on the streets of Capitan with a pistol and fired three shots at him. Whether he was hit is another point of contention, although the *Corona Maverick* states that "the daughter of Bob Hurt shot George Titsworth."[92]

Apparently, a spent bullet hit Titsworth in the ribs, but the powder in the shell was defective and the bullet stopped on his ribs on the left side below the heart, just under the skin.[93] Bessie Hurt was, in turn, arrested and taken to a hearing where she, too, was released. Local lore says that Judge Hudspeth told her, "Young lady, you are free to go. However, had the verdict gone the other way, I was prepared to sentence you to six months of target practice."[94]

Bessie Hurt's nephew, Clarence "Steve" Hilburn, tells the family story of the incident:

> *Another incident to this case was in regard to my Aunt Bessie A. Hurt; she was the daughter of my grandfather and was fifteen years old. She had planned and practiced to shoot George Titsworth for some time. On the day she planned to do this she hid her gun under a cape she was wearing and as she approached him on the street a wind came up exposing her gun. George was able to grab the gun when she pulled the trigger and it grazed him on the shoulder. She did not spend one day in jail, at her arraignment she was asked whether she shot George Titsworth, her reply was "You're damn right I did and I'm sorry I didn't kill the Son-of-a-bitch." It shook up the court and her only sentence was to get out of New Mexico for one year.*[95]

Left: Bessie Hurt, circa 1925. *Photograph courtesy of Clarence Hilburn.*

Below: George A. Titsworth standing in front of the Titsworth Company Store, circa 1940s. *Photograph courtesy of the Karol Schatzel Collection.*

Perhaps the greatest irony of the whole incident is that Robert Hurt had apparently tired of the quarrel. He had sold his ranch and livestock and was preparing to move back to Texas when he was killed, a fact that was common knowledge in the community.

CUMMINS CORPORATION

After George Titsworth passed and his estate had been settled, all of the property was purchased by Will Ed Harris. The Titsworth Store was managed by James Black, starting in 1950. Hollis Cummins, a local youth, started working at the Titsworth Mercantile Company in the summer of 1950, before returning to the University of New Mexico in the fall.

At the end of the spring semester in May 1951, Hollis returned to Capitan, where he became grocery manager of the Titsworth Store. During a conversation one day, Jim Black mentioned that the store would be sold, and Cummins commented that he would like to own the grocery store but had no financing to purchase it. Black approached Cummins later and asked if he was serious about operating the grocery store; he said that if so, some means of financing could be arranged.

Supported by his parents, who offered their property in Capitan as collateral, Cummins met with A.E. Huntsinger of the Citizens Bank of Vaughn and purchased the grocery portion of the Titsworth Store. The dry goods portion was purchased by Manual and Edna Jones of Carrizozo; the hardware store was bought by Bill Nickles, also of Carrizozo; and the Standard Oil dealership was purchased by Dorothy Ferris of Capitan and Mr. and Mrs. Willard Teague of Roswell. Several years later, Cummins purchased the dry good portion of the store from the Joneses. The hardware store was later sold to the Dean family, who operated it until the 1960s. Since that time, it has had a variety of owners and is currently operated as the Lincoln County Mercantile.

After Cummins bought the dry goods portion of the store, his parents assisted him in its operation throughout its early years. Both had worked for Mr. Titsworth, so their experience was invaluable. During the first eight years of operation, Cummins lived with his parents and learned every aspect of the grocery store business, including meat cutting.

Cummins's grandfather, Joseph Cummins, immigrated to the Tucson Mountain northwest of Capitan from Kentucky in 1904 and farmed there until his death in 1932. Joseph's youngest son, Lewis, grew up on the family

Above: The third Titsworth Company Store looking west down Smokey Bear Boulevard, circa 1940. *Photograph from Margie Titsworth Slayton Estate collection.*

Below: Titsworth employees and their families at a Titsworth Company picnic, circa 1940s. *Photograph courtesy of Hollis Cummins.*

ranch and attended school in Capitan, where he graduated in 1921. His wife, Bessie Robertson, grew up in the Eagle Creek area. Both worked in the Titsworth Store, but Lewis later became a teacher after attending New Mexico Normal School in Las Vegas. He eventually became a school principal.

In 1944, Lewis was appointed finance officer for the German internment camp at nearby Fort Stanton. In 1945, the Cummins family leased the Buena Vista Motel, where Bessie cooked meals while Lewis served them. Upon retirement in 1958, Lewis was elected treasurer of Lincoln County for two terms. He had previously served as Capitan village clerk in the 1930s. Lewis and Bessie had three children: Geraldine, Ted and Hollis.

In 1965, a new store was built, behind the third Titsworth Store, that housed the Cummins' Food Market and Dry Goods, as well as the Dean Hardware Store and a new post office. After forty-two years of operation, Hollis's son, David, purchased the Cummins Corporation in 1993 and subsequently sold it to the Farmer's Country Market chain of Roswell in 1997. In 2006, the store was once again sold and became Smokey's Country Market.

CHAPTER 5

THE NORTH SIDE

The Capitan Mountains are an anomaly. They are one of only three or four mountain chains in the United States that run east and west instead of north and south. Small compared to the others, they are a two-mountain chain, nine miles northeast of the village of Capitan, consisting of Capitan Mountain and West Mountain. The mountains are widely thought to be named for Captain Saturnino Baca, a pioneer politician; however, these mountains were named "Sierra Capitan" by Spanish explorers at least as early as 1780. The highest point, Capitan Peak, is 10,083 feet. West Mountain rises to 8,224 feet above sea level. Each mountain is three or four miles wide at the base. Much of the land is contained in the Capitan Mountain Wilderness, created in 1980 and consisting of 35,822 acres. Capitan Gap, at 7,542 vertical feet, is located between the two mountains.

Among the first settlers on the north side were Hispanics, mostly from the Manzano area, who established sheep ranches on the prairies and in mountain canyons. One of these settlements was carved in the middle of the Block Ranch, operated by the Sedillo family.

Although the Eighteenth Amendment to the Constitution prohibited the use of alcohol, bootlegging became prevalent, and this terrain around Capitan, with its rugged canyons and remoteness, was rumored to have supported many stills. Perhaps the most famous site was the "Bloody Bucket," a popular dance hall and reported speakeasy of the early twentieth century, located in the Capitan Gap.

As Capitan grew and evolved into the mercantile center for Lincoln County in the early 1900s, so too did a series of settlements and large ranches on the north side of the mountains. In the last quarter of the nineteenth century, there was a dirt road that ran parallel on the north side of the Capitan Mountains before turning south and running into Capitan once past the end of West Mountain. In the twentieth century, that road was paved and renamed New Mexico Highway 246. Today, it is a narrow two-lane highway running from Capitan to Roswell, and it is rarely taken, except by the local residents.

The remoteness of the north side caused the residents to socialize in an isolated context. Schools and churches became dance halls on weekends. Church services were also held in a variety of places, and picnics were held during the summer months, especially on the Fourth of July, with participants sometimes riding long distances and often spending the night.

Willa Stone noted that the weather on her family's ranch has changed significantly in the past fifty years. She spoke of ample summer rains, which flooded their hay meadows, and winter snows totaling ten to twelve feet annually. Summer would be spent spraying gourd vines and weeds in the native blue gamma grass hay meadows; then the merchant families would bale hay until the fall cattle work began. The cattle were driven cross-country to the Carrizozo stockyards, where the calves were loaded on the train in early October. Creeks that used to run clear water all the time now have slowed to a trickle, or they have run dry. This continual drying of the area's climate drove the homesteaders to leave, as they could no longer sustain dry land farming and small livestock operations.[96]

SETTLEMENTS

Paradise Valley was a short-lived settlement on Carrizo Creek, twelve miles north of Capitan and four miles northwest of Encinoso. The settlement of Deseo, also located here, only existed for about four or five years in the 1920s before it was abandoned due to drought. It had a post office from 1916 to 1918. *Deseo* is Spanish for "I want" or "I desire." The name was given to the settlement by Miss Sarah Aragon, from a prominent local family. The locals built an adobe school in about 1915. The school faced south, with windows to the east and a high window to the north. The walls were ten or twelve feet high, with a round stove in the building. The building was used for church on Sunday and dancing on weekends. The first teacher was a Mrs. Moss.[97]

Water is a priceless commodity, and there are two strong springs in the area and in Gumm Canyon, on the north side of West Mountain. In the late 1800s, a sawmill was built above the canyon, on top of West Mountain. The operator made a round trip to the springs each day with twelve pack mules, each carrying two water kegs, to get water for the sawmill boiler. That sawmill burned down in 1899. In the early 1900s, there were open-faced logs carrying water from the springs down to the settlers in and around Encinoso. Also in the early 1900s, the Encinoso Canyon ran a clear stream of water, carried to Encinoso by way of an open-faced log trough. Local people often walked the log trough, keeping the troughs free of pine needles and other debris. In the late 1800s, an open-faced log trough carried water from the springs in Merchant Canyon to early settlers' homes and farm plots at the base of the mountain. Remnants of these log troughs can still be seen.

Encinoso was once a thriving little settlement thirteen miles northeast of Capitan on New Mexico State Road 246. R.A. Duran and Sam Farmer established a community here for sheepherders working on the Block Ranch, naming it for a stand of oak trees. Encinoso was once known as "the town of fives" because it was reported to have had five bars, five stables and five houses of ill repute. By the early 1950s, there were four homes and

Encinoso School, circa 1950s. *Photograph courtesy of Willa Stone.*

a Catholic church, but little else remains. It had a post office from 1915 to 1920 and also a school, which closed in 1952, with Hattie Lacey serving as the last teacher. Like many other schools in the county, the Encinoso School was one room for grades one through eight, and it also served as a voting place until the mid-1950s.

Above: The Block Ranch Headquarters in Richardson, New Mexico, circa 1900. *Photograph courtesy of Willa Stone.*

Below: Meek Post Office, circa 1910. *Photograph courtesy of Historical Society of South Eastern New Mexico.*

From the Coalora Coal Mines to Smokey Bear

The large Hopkins Ranch was a stopping place on the road between Fort Sumner and Fort Stanton in the 1860s. It was located about twenty-five miles from Fort Stanton, in the foothills of Capitan Mountain. In 1866, the members of the Mescalero Apache tribe murdered several of the ranch hands there. Sadly, the location of Hopkins Ranch has been lost to history.

Richardson, a settlement at the headquarters of the Block Ranch, had a post office from 1895 to 1912, and it also had a school. The abandoned settlement was named for Andrew Richardson, one of the managers of the El Capitan Land and Cattle Company and also the first postmaster. There is a public cemetery here. Early local settlers also called Richardson by the name *Las Norias*, meaning "the wells" in Spanish.

Meek was a settlement on the northeast side of the Capitan Mountains at the mouth of Arroyo Seco Canyon, eight miles from Arabella, and it housed a post office from 1904 to 1922. Now abandoned, it took its name from the first postmaster, Thomas B. Meek. For a limited time, there was also a stage stop and school here, where area ranchers came for weekend and holiday dances.

Las Tablas was a small Hispanic settlement on the north side of the Capitan Mountains near Seven Cabins. The name means "the boards" or "the planks," perhaps from a sawmill operated there. It was a reported hideout of Billy the Kid and the site of many local dances. The U.S. census of 1900 showed its population as 242. Virtually no trace of this community remains today.

About 1885, Antonio Montoya migrated to Las Tablas from his birthplace in Valencia County and ranched in the area for the rest of his life. The 1900 census shows a family of four sons and two daughters. On December 11, 1923, Montoya and his extended family left Las Tablas for Jarales in the Manzano Mountains to attend a wedding. Traveling by wagons, the group stopped to rest as they neared their destination. A storm suddenly developed and quickly turned into a full-scale blizzard. During the night, family members succumbed to the cold until only Antonio and his son Juan were left alive. The pair set out for help. Antonio was rescued but lost his left foot and several fingers. Juan was never seen again. Antonio died a year later due to his injuries from the storm.[98]

Seven Cabins, a small group of seven cabins above Peach Tree Canyon on the north side of the Capitan Mountains, was founded about 1860, but the area was abandoned by the 1880s. The seven cabins ran in a north–south line, and all have vanished. There was a rumor that the cabins were a hideout for outlaws and that buried treasure was found here; another theory is that a polygamist built the cabins, with each cabin housing a wife.

Spindle, a settlement on the north side of the Capitan Mountains, twenty-two miles northeast of Capitan, housed a post office from 1917 to 1920 and also a school. One residence remains at the settlement, but this general area of Lincoln County is still called Spindle. A highway sign currently marks its location on State Road 246. Spindle had a one-room school consisting of grades one through eight before 1920. The building was constructed of clapboard and painted white, and in front of the building was a belfry. The rear had a cistern to catch rainwater and two separate outhouses for girls and boys. During this time, school was taught by a Miss Alta.[99]

The tiny Hispanic community of Las Palas is located in the vicinity of Arabella on the northeast side of the Capitan Mountains. The name means "the shovels" in Spanish.

Pine Lodge, a settlement on the northeast side of the Capitan Mountains, thirty-two miles northeast of Capitan and three miles south of New Mexico State Road 246, was the site of a tuberculosis sanitarium and later a summer resort, constructed in 1909. In the early 1920s, the Boy Scouts had a summer camp here; hence, nearby Boy Scout Mountain is named as a landmark to the southwest of the settlement. From 1939 to the mid-1940s, Pine Lodge was operated by the James Edgar family, including a lodge, café, cabins and dormitories where families could spend summers, vacations and weekends.

Pine Lodge in 1922. This was probably a special-use-permit guest facility. *Photograph by J.D. Jones, FS #178074, courtesy of U.S. Forest Service.*

Many dances were held, attended by people from surrounding communities. The lodge burned in 1980 and again during the Peppin Fire in 2004, which burned almost the entire eastern end of the mountain. Only seven cabins were left standing. Scattered cabins remain today.

Lon was originally settled by James and Joneta Bagley and named Raw Hide Flat. The Bagleys opened a general mercantile store and operated a post office from 1934 to 1943. In the back of the mercantile was a school, which held nine or ten students taught by Miss Callie Franks. The abandoned community originally was named "Joneta" for Mrs. Joneta Bagley. In 1931, the post office was taken over by Jerome and Minnie Mosley, and the name changed to "Lon" for the son of postmaster Ben Mosley. Another opinion holds that the settlement might have been named for Lon Merchant, a local rancher. Miss Franks returned to Texas, and a two-room school was built by the Mosleys that taught fifteen to twenty-five students. In 1941, the school was closed, and the students went to Corona. In 1943, Mosley closed the store in a dispute with the federal government and moved to Oregon.

Bethel was the name of a school located on Highway 246, on the northeast side of the Capitan Mountains. Sometimes Bethel was known as "Hogwaller," after being called that by an unknown cowboy. The name "Bethel" was given to the site by schoolteacher Ida June Rector. The school burned down in 1929 but was later rebuilt and moved to the Purcella Ranch.

The final area on the "north side" is Arroyo Macho. Located on the plains northeast of the Capitan Mountains, it is an inhospitable land where water is intermittent at best. It has seen some of the best cattle ranching in the area, most prominently by Ed and John Downing. Sometime about 1915, the settlers in the Arroyo Macho area decided there were enough school age children in the area to start a school. "Pa" Davis and Guy Crandall drove the family Model T Ford to the county seat in Carrizozo and requested that a school be established at Spindle. The county superintendent agreed to furnish the teacher's salary and books for the students, but the local ranchers had to agree to provide a schoolhouse and a place for the teacher to live. Dan McFarland provided an old building used to store feed, and a Miss Tonia Vandebout from Dexter was hired as the teacher.[100]

CHAPTER 6

RANCHING CONCERNS

R anching has always been the primary occupation on the north side of the Capitan Mountains, and rightfully so. Rarely has better country been found for ranching, and that tradition continues today with many multigenerational families carrying on the proud traditions of their ancestors.

HUNT RANCH

Sometime around 1900, George Hunt bought a ranch at the foot of Capitan Mountain with two strong natural springs on it. The family eventually split their time equally each year between the ranch and a house in the village of Lincoln. Pansy Hunt tells of moving to the area on the north side of the Capitan Mountains and of building the ranch house:

> *Then we bought the ranch, just the water rights. You bought your water rights, and that was two springs that ran out of the mountains, everlasting, they never dried up, they're still going yet. And then you allowed the 350 acres for school land. I don't know why they called it school land but they did. And you could fence that to run your saddle horses in or whatever you wanted in there. It was a beautiful place—the Capitan Range of the mountains—it was. There was no foothills, therefore the mountains came right out onto the prairie. All free-range country. Didn't cost a penny to run your stock, if you could furnish the water, get water for them. So that is what we did.*

Then from there we was in the sheep business from that time the whole ten years that we lived there. The first year that we were there—we settled in the mountains along about the first part of September. Then it took them—it took about a year before we got the house made. Now the logs— the trees—the pine trees, they were cut down. They were hewn. They were skinned and they took all the bark off of them. They were flattened on two sides and then notched on the ends. We had a man who knew what we were doing on this, to make them. And it was a large house. It was an awful big place. And it took a year before we got moved into this place. Course the house was made in a u-shape so there was a good patio, good sized. I would say there was at least twenty-foot square or maybe a little more than that. And there was a tree right in the very center of that. A very beautiful cedar tree. The house was built right around that cedar tree. And I might just say now that I saw it forty-four years after I left there—I was back and saw it forty-four years after I left there—I was back and saw it and it is one of the most monstrous trees there is around the country, because it got good water all the time.

We piped the water down the mountains—a mile and a half and ten rods—to be exact. I had to ride it a few times in the dark and it scared the liver out of me. Because the furtherest one up (spring) was right down, just almost felt like you could nearly reach from one mountain to the other side, because it was right at the bottom of the rock slide.[101]

Pansy continues the story of the settlement of the Hunt Ranch, describing the water system:

Now this was an open pipe now, made out of four 1x4's, wood, open top, you couldn't put a pipe in because they'd (the animals) close it up, you couldn't. And then all the water would stop like that...

The first year we went we had cattle. But that didn't work. They wasn't doing any good, and then we bought four thousand head of sheep the next year. Never owned a sheep in his life [her father] before that. Started out with four thousand head and it took the whole family but me and Mother and little sister and I had to take care of that. So it was my business to keep the water open.[102]

Hunt sold the ranch to Charles Spence, who ranched there until 1910, when he sold it to John and Jim Mocho.

MOCHO RANCH

Two immigrant brothers from the Basque area of France established a significant ranch in the foothills of the Capitan Mountains shortly after the turn of the last century. John and Jean "Jim" Mocho moved to near Encinoso in the fall of 1910 to establish a ranch for sheep. The initial ranch, formerly the Charles Spence ranch, sat on 160 acres of deeded land, had two good springs and a permit to graze two thousand ewes during summer months on Forest Service Land.

Two years later, in 1912, the Mocho brothers had saved enough money through good business and management of their sheep to significantly expand their ranch. Jim's son Pete describes that purchase.

> *Many things changed when the Territory became a State. The lands, once open lands, acquired some government controls. A new dimension of responsibility fell on Dad and Uncle John if they were to hold claim to what they had acquired. Their lack of knowledge in such matters benefitted from political competition between the Democrats and Republicans who had seen to the territory becoming a state. The first elected Governor of the*

John (right) and Jean "Jim" Mocho, circa 1910. *Photograph courtesy of Jim Mocho.*

State of New Mexico was Mr. W. "Bill" McDonald, a Democrat and neighboring rancher, owner of the Block Ranch, who Dad and Uncle John regarded as a strong competitor for the open range land.

They maintained good relations with the people who managed the Block Ranch, and spoke highly of manager Truman A. Spencer and Lloyd Taylor, the foreman. They were sociable and shared work times with each other. In Lincoln County, the republicans, under leadership of Mr. Andrew Hudspeth, a lawyer, and Mr. Charles Spence, a banker, seized on the opportunity of limiting Governor McDonald's expansion of his Block Ranch by taking Dad and Uncle John to Santa Fe and helping them file on state range land and against Governor McDonald's expansion of his Block Ranch. This was possible because land ownership was the needed authority to file on adjacent tracts of public lands. Dad and Uncle John, with the purchase of the old Spanish tract, were the only landowners near Governor McDonald who were authorized to claim a commensurate right to the new state lands. The result of this assistance, for political reasons, enabled Dad and Uncle John to block up a ranch totaling over 160.000 acres of choice land in the central part of Lincoln County.[103]

The Mocho brothers prospered during the next five years, and soon other ranchers moved into the area and settled between the Mochos and the Block Ranch. One evening in 1913, John came in and told his brother Jim that he had met the most beautiful girl he had ever seen and had spent the day at the neighboring ranch of Thomas Shoemaker. On April 2, 1914, John married Nora Shoemaker. Shortly thereafter, Jim started dating Ora Shoemaker, whom he married on July 3, 1916. John's wife, Nora (Shoemaker), describes the house they lived in:

There was a eight room log house on this ranch which had a porch that ran sixty-one feet along the north side. The logs were hand hewn, native pine. Some of them were thirty feet long and eighteen inches thick at the heavy end. Three of the rooms were 18 by 24 feet. The house was U shaped, and the two wings of the house enclosed a patio with a big juniper tree in the center. The south side of the house was on ground level, but the north side with the porch was six feet above the ground. To me, it was a very, very interesting building. It was at the edge of the forest and nice gamma grass prairie as far as the eye could see to the north. Water from a mountain stream was piped down to the place and a part came through the house.

Original homestead building constructed about 1895 and used by the Hunt, Mocho and Merchant families, circa 1930s. *Photograph courtesy of Willa Stone.*

Another spring piped water to an irrigation tank east of the corrals where ten peach trees provided fruit from July through October, and a grape arbor grew different kinds of grapes.[104]

The house had been built in the 1890s, probably by George Hunt and his sons, who owned the ranch prior to Charles Spence. The date "September 1896" is carved above the door of the north wing. With the house being built in a U shape, John Mocho and his family occupied one wing, and Jim Mocho occupied the other wing. The "cold room" was at the base of the U and was the room the stream ran through to keep things cold.

Eventually the two families outgrew the house and could not agree how to divide the land. In 1917, the brothers went to Roswell on a Tuesday and came home on Wednesday. On Saturday, they met their "commissioned seller" coming from Capitan with a buyer, who looked over the ranch on Saturday afternoon and Sunday, and they sold the whole operation on Monday for cash to Pete Etcheverry and George Walker. In the ten years they had owned the ranch, it had grown to eight hundred head of cattle and ten thousand ewes. The cows brought eighty dollars a head and the sheep fourteen dollars each.[105]

MERCHANT RANCH

The Merchant Ranch is fourteen miles north of Capitan along Highway 246 and runs from the base of West Capitan Mountain north to the rolling plains. When purchased by Wallace and Hattie Merchant in August 1925 from Pete and Josepha Etcheverry, the 9,160-acre (fourteen section) ranch consisted of Isidro McKinley's land, Jim and John Mocho's land and Pete Etcheverry's land.

The Merchants' sons' families, Lon (L.D.) and Ruby and "Bug" (J.L.) and Marguerite, settled on the ranch with them. Lon and Ruby's daughters, Marie and Margie, attended school in the area—Margie attended Capitan, where she was the valedictorian of her senior class, while Marie lived with family friends and attended school in Roswell so that she could continue violin lessons and further her musical interests. Through the years, as the north side became more arid and homesteads less viable, Lon purchased homesteads and small plots of land, until the ranch reached approximately eighty sections.

Lon built a log home near the older U-shaped ranch headquarters, but it and the family's possessions were destroyed in 1948 by a fire thought to be started during a lightning storm. John Emdee, a local contractor, built a spacious block home in the very same location that same year. Lon was president of the Southeastern New Mexico Cattle Growers Association for twenty-six years and served on the Capitan School Board.

After marrying a Block cowboy by the name of Grady Eldridge in 1939, Margie Merchant and Grady joined the ranch in 1940. They built a home in the late 1940s on the northern reaches of the ranch and lived at that location until their deaths. Grady Eldridge received a waiver from the military during World War II and managed both the Block and Merchant Ranches. He didn't even brand the cattle because there were so few cowboys who didn't go to war. Grady's son, Ronnie, was killed in a pickup accident, and his son Grady Le died after a grassfire at the young age of twenty-three. A daughter, Betsy Eldridge Peralta, teaches at Capitan Schools and lives nearby. Sons of Grady Le and Melanie Eldridge, Ronnie and Teke, currently own and operate the north portion of Merchant Ranch, now the Eldridge Ranch.

In 1939, the local mail carrier from Pine Lodge, Bill Edgar, met Marie Merchant on the mail route. They married in December 1942 at Fort Hood, Texas. After the war, the couple returned to Bill's home at Pine Lodge in 1946, joining the Merchant family ranch in 1948. Bill served on the Capitan School Board and Lincoln County Fair Board for many years, as well as the Roswell Production Credit Board and the Otero County Electric Board. Marie passed away in 1989 and Bill in 1998. They are buried in the Capitan Cemetery.

The Edgars' daughter, Willa, born in 1949, grew up living in the old Mocho headquarters, the U-shaped house. After graduating from New Mexico State University, she married Preston Stone Jr., who grew up on the adjoining Block Ranch where his father, Preston Sr., managed the ranch. Preston served in the army during Vietnam. Upon his return, Preston managed ranches near Vaughn and Pastura, with Willa teaching high school at Vaughn. Then, in the summer of 1972, the couple was called home to the Merchant/Edgar Ranch due to Bill's health. Willa taught high school science at Carrizozo for seven years, from 1972 to 1979. Troy and Tracey were born in 1976. Troy married Kimberly Smith and returned to the family ranch in 2006 to live in the old Hunt House with their sons, Eleck and Bryce, the sixth generation of the family to live on the ranch. Tracey lives in Bitterroot Valley, Montana.

SHOEMAKER RANCH

One of the early settlers on the north side of the Capitan Mountains was Thomas H. Shoemaker, born near Quitman, Texas, in 1860. Shoemaker married Emily Cannon from Georgia. The family wandered around Texas before immigrating to Lincoln County by way of Oklahoma and eastern New Mexico. The Shoemaker family had eleven children by the time they settled in Lincoln County. Arriving on the north side of the Capitan Mountains about 1911, Thomas built a homestead at the edge of the forest near a natural spring and had a canyon named after him.

The Thomas Shoemaker family in 1902. *Children standing from left to right*: Nora Odessa, Osciola, Olin and Oliver. Parents: Emily Cannon Shoemaker and Thomas Shoemaker. *Children seated in front row*: Ora, Ottman, Otto, Ottice and Oscar. Orton and Orval were yet to be born. *Photograph courtesy of Jim Mocho.*

Shoemaker's daughter Odessa "Nora" married nearby rancher John Mocho, and her sister Ora married Jim Mocho. About 1920, Emily took the remaining family, with the exception of son Otman, and moved away from the ranch.

Thomas had several disputes with the Forest Service over grazing allotments and is suspected of setting a forest fire on U.S. Forest Service land in 1927. The result of the fire was the death of Shoemaker and forest ranger W.C. White in a shootout and the burning of a large amount of forest on Forest Service land. Otman continued to live on the ranch after Thomas's death. Emily outlived Thomas by seven years and died while visiting son Oscar in California in 1934.

BLOCK RANCH

The Block Ranch existed in various forms in New Mexico and the Southwest. At its zenith, it included other ranch ventures, such as the Bar W Ranch, and business entities such as the El Capitan Land and Cattle Company, Tres Ritos Ranch Company, Three Rivers Land and Livestock Company, Quatros Amigos Cattle Company and Carrizozo Cattle Company.[106]

At one time, the Block Ranch was one of the largest ranches in the Southwest, yet its first occupants were members of the Jornada Mogollon tribe rather than cowboys. During the 1950s, Jane Holden Kelley excavated a Jornada Mogollon pueblo site on one of the highest areas of the ranch. Because of its location on the hill, the twenty-room, double-row pueblo is described as a defensive site, one of the few such sites found in the cultural area. Though the site was occupied earlier, the pueblo dates from AD 1340 to 1370.[107]

The Block Ranch, also known as "the Blocks" or "Three Block Ranch," was established after the Civil War but sometime before 1871, when it was sold by a John Kirk for $100, two axes, one pit of cabbage, one scythe and sneathe, one bedstead, two sacks full of corn (not shelled), two small sacks of beans, one pitchfork and two hoes. The property was sold again in 1873. Several other sales occurred during this time frame that included the large spring at the Cienega del Macho. In May 1879, John C. DeLaney, post sutler at Fort Stanton, submitted a land application for a Desert Land Entity.[108]

The defining moment for the ranch occurred when it was incorporated in 1885 as the El Capitan Land and Cattle Company by Andrew and Melvin Richardson, John DeLaney and Horace and Charles Thurber. Andy Richardson, who arrived in the area about 1869, soon emerged as the manager, and he guided the ranch through its rapid rise. Richardson married Maria

"Benina" Lucero from Arabella, and the couple eventually had six children. It was Andrew Richardson's horse that Billy the Kid stole after escaping from Lincoln on his way to Fort Sumner. The ranch eventually sold to Charles Thurber, and Richardson moved to Kansas, where he died in 1905.

The Thurbers managed the ranch from afar and actually never came to it. The ranch was managed by a man named Steele who might have been related to the Thurbers. Either the Thurbers or Richardsons established a store at the ranch headquarters to provide supplies for the Block cowboys and their families. The ranch headquarters, the store and a post office were designated "Richardson."

The Thurbers were bought out by an English consortium. There is also some indication that a Stephenson Commission Company in Kansas City partnered with the English consortium. When the Thurbers sold the ranch, a restrictive covenant was added to allow all of the Hispanic sheepherders on the north side the use of the Block Ranch water and springs. William McDonald managed the ranch for the absent owners in England and Kansas City.

About 1909, the ranch was sold to William McDonald's Bar W Ranch in Carrizozo for $250,000. In the years 1908–11, the ranch sold half a million dollars' worth of cattle to the Stephensons in Kansas City. McDonald managed the ranch until his death in 1918.

The ranch was located on the northern side of the Capitan Mountains and extended west and south to Carrizozo and beyond. At one time, it was reported to have a drift fence stretching north from the Capitan Mountains to Vaughn. It was said to be at least five hundred sections in size and ran an estimated sixty-five thousand head of cattle. Into the first part of the twentieth century, the ranch still covered 96,000 acres. At its zenith, it was reported to be 160,000 acres, but no one knows for sure. In 1982, John Sinclair wrote: "It was told around Capitan fifty years ago that in the early years of the Block Ranch, cattle of the brand grazed from the Rio Pecos to the Rio Grande, an east-to-west, crow-flight distance of 160 miles."[109]

Carlton Britton whose father, Nathaniel Britton, was foreman of the ranch, writes of the ranch's history:

The El Capitan Land and Cattle Company hired a bookkeeper in the 1880s named W.C. McDonald. Over the years McDonald gradually bought out all the partners and by 1908 was the sole owner of the Block Ranch. In the old west it was not uncommon for the bookkeeper to end up with the ranch. McDonald became the first Governor of the State of New

Mexico in 1912 and was obviously a man of great drive and intelligence. As McDonald became more involved in New Mexico politics, he hired a bookkeeper named Truman Spencer. True to the bookkeeper pattern, Spencer became the owner of the Block Ranch, but his method was simple, he ran off with the governor's daughter. The ranch stayed in the McDonald-Spencer family until it sold in 1949 to Mr. Wassham who bought it for his son to operate. Evidently the son had little interest in ranching. Wassham sold the ranch to Tobe Foster, an oilman and trader from Lubbock, Texas, in 1950. Actually, Tobe paid Wassham for his original payment to Truman Spencer but in fact bought the ranch from Spencer. At this time, the Blocks comprised of some 150 sections with a forest permit of about 50 sections or about 128,000 acres.

Tobe Foster died in 1956 and the ranch operated under the guidance of several administrators, primarily Walter Clark of Lubbock, G.H. Heyward of Big Spring and Truman Sanders, an attorney from Roswell. In 1959, the administrators sold the ranch to D.D. Bruton, and his wife Laura Lu, from Dallas, Texas. With Mr. Bruton's health failing, they sold the ranch in 1964 to the Cannings. [110]

Nathalee Britton Taylor, who grew up on the ranch when her father was foreman there, puts the ranch's size in a different perspective: "I would not even hazard a guess as to how big it was, but in the late nineteenth and early twentieth centuries, there were 65,000 cattle on the Block range. They had five chuck wagons, and they stayed out all of the time. They had ten cowboys per wagon and five hundred saddle horses. They just branded and branded." [111]

Perhaps the most amazing part of the ranch was the drift fence that caught the cattle on the west side of the ranch. The Block's drift fence ran from the Capitan Mountains in the south north for seventy or eighty miles to Vaughn. It was built so well that posts from it are still standing today.

Hap Canning bought the ranch in 1964 and owned it until his death in the early 2000s. The ranch was split and sold in 2009, with each part a substantial ranch in its own right.

BLOCK COWBOYS

George Curry, the last territorial governor of New Mexico, was a Block cowboy in the 1880s. He told of a night in 1880 when he was visited at a Block line cabin by a polite young man. As was the custom, Curry cooked

Block Ranch cowboys at Block Ranch Headquarters, circa 1930s. The cowboy on the left on the white horse is Montana Clark; the large man in the middle of the photograph is Lloyd Taylor, the Block manager for years; and second from the right is Grady Eldridge. *Photograph courtesy of Carlton Britton.*

supper for the stranger, and they talked of local politics. It was only after the man rode off without telling Curry his name that local sheepherders told him his visitor was Billy the Kid.[112]

Other notable Block cowboys were Red Dale, Roy Roddy, John Lacey, Arthur "Montana" Clark and John and Ed Downing.

Mrs. T.C. Key writes, "One day [in 1901] a man came…and talked to my brother. As the man was leaving my brother turned to me and said, 'That is Jack Thorp, the man who wrote "Little Joe the Wrangler."'"[113] Later in life, Mrs. Key was again in contact with Thorp, when he wrote to her asking for her help with an ongoing copyright battle over who had really written the famous cowboy ballad.

The Block Ranch had many cowboys over the years, but perhaps one of the most famous was Nathan Howard "Jack" Thorp. Thorp was born in New York City in 1867. As the son of a prominent attorney, he spent his early years in the elite social circles of New York and Philadelphia. In the summer, he lived on his brother's ranch in Nebraska, and by the time he was in his late teens, he knew how to ride a horse. Moving to New Mexico, he worked as a cowboy on the Block Ranch before buying his own ranch.

Jack Thorp was more than just a cowboy—he was the first person to collect and publish the songs of the cowboys sung on the range. He began his journey in 1899 and traveled 1,500 miles in twelve states before he walked into the *Estancia News* office in 1908 and paid to have two thousand copies of his book of "cowboy songs" published for six cents each. The final product was bound in red and contained twenty-three songs in fifty pages.

While Thorp collected songs from cowboys throughout the Southwest, perhaps the best-known song in that volume was his own song "Little Joe the Wrangler." He also wrote "Three Block Tom," whose tale centers on the Block Ranch, with its title referring to the brand of the Block Ranch. Jack Thorp had begun the acceptance of the genre of western music.[114]

The Brill Ranch is about thirty-five miles north of Capitan and south of Highway 246. Nick and Mary Brill bought the original ranch located near McHallis Canyon from homesteader Reuben Michaelis in 1909. When their daughter Dorothy turned five, they homesteaded and established the "lower ranch" near the "Hogwaller" (Bethel) School so Dorothy could attend elementary school. The ranch remains under family management by daughter Dorothy Epps, age ninety-four, and great-granddaughter Mary Folkner.

The Bird Ranch, forty-one miles northeast of Capitan on Highway 246, was founded in 1917 when R.G. and Bess Bird homesteaded on the Serrano Creek, fifteen miles east of Pine Lodge. Later on, they built an adobe house a mile east of the original homestead. Son R.G. "Buster" Bird Jr. and wife Jerry lived at the ranch for a time after the elder Birds retired from ranching. Buster stayed at the ranch, and Jerry taught school in Roswell. After Buster retired, son Bill took over the ranching operation in 1976. Bill and his wife, Sharon, continue to manage the ranch today.

The Purcella Ranch, also known as T75 Ranch, on Serrano Creek is about forty-one miles northeast of Capitan on Highway 246. It was established in 1932, when Louis Purcella proved up a 640-acre homestead after the family had lived there since the early 1900s. Louis and his wife, Betty (Annie Elizabeth), added to the ranch until it was seven sections.

Upon Louis's death in 1939, son John and his wife, Nettie, purchased the original seven-section ranch. The couple built perimeter fencing and developed a watering system with storage tanks and many miles of water pipelines to water the ranch, which ran sheep. They, too, added to the ranch's size, buying other homesteads and land until the ranch totaled twenty-three sections. Due to advancing age and a changing economy and sheep market, John and Nettie sold all the sheep and converted to cattle about 1960.

John and Nettie retired from the ranch in 1971 and moved into Roswell, leaving the ranch management in the hands of their daughter, Jeanette Smoot, and her husband, Buster. After Buster's death, the ranch remains in the hands of Jeanette Smoot and daughters Minette Harper and Sharon Bird.

One of the ranches most distant from Capitan on the north side was the Downing Ranch owned by brothers John and Ed Downing. Born in Texas, the brothers worked on the Block Ranch after serving in World War I, where John worked with cattle and Ed was a renowned chuck wagon cook. Guy Crandall described John Downing and the work of a chuck wagon cook:

> *After the cowboys had been fed and gone off on the morning cattle drive, John Downing's work had just begun. While John went about loading camping gear, his flunky and the horse wrangler harnessed the workhorses. When all was ready, John climbed on the wagon seat and grasped the ribbons with which he guided the four-horse-team. With a yelp, he slapped their rumps, setting into motion the chuck wagon followed by the wood wagon and, off to one side, the trotting horse herd. The night before Lloyd Taylor had designated the next campsite and cattle holding ground, which was down the draw several miles near a waterhole.*[115]

While working on the Block Ranch, the Downing brothers saved their money and bought out failing ranches. They eventually acquired some fourteen

"Chuck and Chat" at Purcella Ranch, taken circa 1950s. *From left to right*: Nick Brill, Ed Downing, Walter Jones, Lloyd Hale (seated), Bob Lathum, Lon Merchant, unknown, John Downing and Bill Edgar. *Photograph courtesy of Willa Stone.*

sections of land that included state and federal allotments with headquarters thirty-five miles northeast of Capitan on the Macho Creek. On this range they ran one thousand sheep, three hundred Hereford cows, thirty-five Angora goats and thirty horses. Both brothers retired from ranching and moved to Lincoln. John died in 1954, and Ed followed in 1959. Both are buried in the Capitan Cemetery.

Many of the ranchers "on the north side" were active in "Chuck and Chat," in which a group of ranching families met each month to have "chuck" and to "chat." Participants included Ruby and Lon Merchant, Estelle and Bob Latham, John and Ed Downing, Margie and Grady Eldridge, Nettie and John Purcella, Mary and Nick Brill and Charles and Carrie French. Also participating were Margie and Floyd Hale, Marie and Bill Edgar, Bess and Buster Bird, Jeanette and Buster Smoot, Biddy and Francis Owens, Essie and Walter Jones, Nathaniel and Pauline Britton and Eleanor and Charles Jones.

CHAPTER 7

THE U.S. FOREST SERVICE AND THE CIVILIAN CONSERVATION CORPS

The Lincoln Forest Reserve was founded on July 26, 1902, and included much of the Capitan, Vera Cruz and White Mountains in Lincoln County. The forest was established in response to the Reclamation Service and the Texas legislature regarding the forest watershed. The primary purpose was to protect and conserve the water necessary for the success of the Hondo project.[116]

New Mexico forest superintendent I.B. Hanna made a tour of the new Forest Reserve in late 1902. In an bold statement written before New Mexico became a state and when open range was the rule of the land, the *Capitan Progress* quoted Hanna as saying:

> *There is a great deal of abuse to the timber on the reserve and the government will have it stopped…it is a case of preserving the forest for posterity and future generations. Many persons have committed depredations and they are hard to head off suddenly, but we can accomplish this in time. They are those who believe the government control of the forest is an interference in their affairs, as they have always been accustomed to doing as they pleased in the wood…*[117]

A few years later, Congressman B.S. Rodney took exception to that concept when he wrote to the commissioner of the General Land Office:

> *I do most solemnly protest against this creating forest reserves in the night without notice to the people…It will not do to tell us that the department*

knows best what we want…all of the fine land included in this new reserve is now taken out of land from which we might make our selections.[118]

Rodney's torch was taken up on June 6, 1906, when the *White Oaks Outlook* wrote:

These reserves will be alright provided the order of the Secretary of the Interior establishing grazing fees is set aside by the courts. Otherwise it will follow heavily on Lincoln County…Homesteaders are not apt to settle inside of these green pastures even if permitted, where they will be compelled to herd their little bunch of cattle or sheep on their own ground, or be fined for turning them loose on government land.[119]

Initially there were nine ranger districts to provide support for the administration of the Forest Reserve: White Mountain/Mesa Ranger District located on the Nogal Mesa founded in 1908; the Ruidoso District at Glencoe, founded in 1907; the Tucson located in the Tucson Mountains, founded in 1911; the Block Station on the Block Ranch at Richardson, founded in 1911; the Baca Site at the Baca Civilian Conservation Corps (CCC) camp, founded in 1907; the North Gallinas at Progresso, founded in 1911; the South Gallinas at Holloway, founded in 1911; and the Patos District in the Patos Mountains, founded in 1911.

The South and North Gallinas were transferred to the Cibola Forest, the Glencoe was closed and moved to the White Mountain and Mesa Station in 1929 and the Patos and Tucson Stations were closed and moved to the White Mountain and Mesa Station. The Block and Baca Stations were closed and moved to Capitan in 1929. Finally, the White Mountain and Mesa Station was closed and moved to a new station in Ruidoso in 1958, as was the Capitan office in 1973. The sole remaining office in Ruidoso was renamed the Smokey Bear Ranger District in 1973.

CAPITAN OFFICE, LINCOLN FOREST RESERVE[120]

The Department of the Interior could not have found a better place to establish its office for the Lincoln Forest Reserve in 1902 than Capitan. Capitan was in the geographical center of both the county and the new forest reserve, and the newly established village was equidistant between the railroad at Carrizozo and the county seat at Lincoln. Additionally, it was quickly becoming the distribution center for the region. In October 1902, forty-year-old frontiersman

Clement Hightower, a Forest Service ranger working on the upper Gila, was promoted to ranger second class and sent to Capitan to become the first Forest Service official working on the Lincoln National Forest.

Born in Arkansas in 1858 and orphaned at an early age, Hightower went first to Colorado and then to New Mexico before settling in the Tularosa River area in western New Mexico. While there, he married Nympha Romero Hayes. He drifted between jobs until 1901, when he was appointed a forest guard on the Gila Forest Reserve and was posted to the area near his Frisco boyhood home.

Initially leaving his family in place, Hightower rented a modest home in Capitan that required a lot of maintenance for six dollars a month. Hightower soon moved his family to the house on a salary of seventy-five dollars per month and a one dollar per diem. However, he had to provide his own horse and pack animals, as well as their feed, and his workday went from sunup to sundown.

Hightower operated at first out of a building in the rear of the post office, but when the weather got warmer, he moved out onto reserve land. In April 1903, he moved into a two-room log cabin five miles northwest of Captain and a mile and half from Coalora and the nearest post office. His office was a similar cabin next to the residence, presumably built and then abandoned by a homesteader.

In a report to the land office dated December 29, 1902, Hightower noted sixty-six thousand sheep and goats and nineteen thousand cattle and horses on the 380,000 acres of reserve land, which did not include Sierra Blanca. He also noted that the ranges were badly overgrazed and recommended that the area be reduced by one-third and grazing limited to 20 acres per head of cattle and 4⅜ acres for each sheep or goat. The commissioner accepted Hightower's recommendation and for 1903 fixed the permit numbers to forty thousand sheep and goats and twelve thousand cattle and horses.

Hightower made other recommendations, including limiting the number of animals in a herd to 1,500 and putting an end to roving herds by distant owners. He began to write a weekly column in the local newspaper, addressing every aspect of the administration of the Federal Reserve. He also publicized the rules of the reserve in both English and Spanish.

A large part of Hightower's time focused on illegal activities such as unauthorized grazing and the cutting of trees for fenceposts and firewood. In one month alone, he found four flocks of 10,000 sheep grazing illegally on the north side of the Capitan Mountains and 3,260 head grazing on the east end of the Capitans. Most woodcutting seemed to be on the east end of the Capitans, which was within easy traveling distance from Roswell and Chaves County.

By March 1903, it was apparent that Hightower needed help, and Ernest Wright was appointed as a forest assistant. Later that month, Hightower requested three more men be appointed to help him manage the Lincoln Forest Reserve, writing, "I respectfully recommend the appointment of three additional men…the sheep men…will require watching…there is continual depredation upon timber…and there is at this time damage from fires…"[121]

In May 1903, Hightower requested a promotion to superintendent, which was granted in June, and he was given a raise to $1,200 per year. However, his $1 per diem had been abolished, so this was a net loss of $5 per month.

Also in 1903, the rangers were instructed to wear uniforms. Since there was no national standard, Hightower soon wrote to a Philadelphia uniform manufacturer requesting uniforms be made "for myself and Forest Rangers under me." The uniform he requested consisted of Bedford cord khaki and a double-breasted coat, square cut with padded shoulders, with nickered or bronzed buttons, three on each sleeve. The vest was to be low cut with a rolled collar, four buttons and two outside pockets; the pants, cavalry style with five pockets; the shirt, olive green with pearl buttons; and the hat, a Stetson with a three-inch brim.[122]

By November of that year, his relations with locals had improved, and except for a couple of sheepherders, the rules of the forest were being complied with. In the case of the cattlemen, he filled allotments with small owners first and the remainder with the big cattle ranchers—the only reserve in the country to do so. Timber was mostly in the form of fencepost and cordwood, and several small sawmills operated on the reserve. During this time Hightower was also charged with verifying homesteads in the forest as allowed by the Homestead Act. In many cases, the homestead had been filed on remotely by people who had never seen the area or even entered the claim. By the end of 1903, Hightower was allowed to employ a second ranger part time.

For years, the Capitan area had been plagued by forest fires, with the last one of significant proportions in 1895. Due to Hightower's actions, local attention was focused on small man-made fires, and this occurrence was greatly reduced.

By 1904, the staff had grown to four assistants, and Hightower recommended establishing an official ranger station in Capitan. In his request he pointed out that his office had only two rooms, and the dirt roof was leaking. Since the Coalora mines were closing, Hightower assured his supervisors that he could rent an office and residence for eight dollars per month. His application was approved, and he was also allowed office furniture and the lease of a

Lincoln Forest Reserve building in Capitan, circa 1905. The Welch store is in the background. Perhaps one of the men in the picture is Clement Hightower. *Photograph courtesy of David Cunningham, Smokey Bear State Park.*

typewriter. He also requested a light vehicle, but the Forest Service did not approve motorized transportation for some years to come.

In a picture dated 1905 (but probably taken in the winter of 1906), the original Capitan Federal Building is shown on the west side of Highway 48 in the block south of Highway 380 where the village hall is located today. Pictured is the building with a gabled roof flying the American flag. In the background is a mercantile building that is almost certainly the original Titsworth Store. Two men stand in front of the building. One wonders if one of them is Clement Hightower.

In December 1904, all forest personnel were transferred to civil service and required to take a test in Santa Fe or Silver City. Hightower and his four rangers passed their tests and, in July 1905, were officially commissioned into the Forest Service.

Clement Hightower's service as supervisor abruptly ended on February 1, 1906. On February 13, Capitan's Spanish-language newspaper *El Farol* wrote:

> *Changes in the Forest Reserve. A change has been made in the Lincoln Forest Reserve, Supervisor Clement Hightower and Forest Guard G.L. Bradford have resigned their employment. Their successors are John Kerr*

of the Gila Reserve, Supervisor, and Paul Griffith F. Angus, Forest Guard in place of Mr. Bradford. Pending the arrival of Mr. Kerr, Coert DuBois, Inspector of Reserves, will be in charge of business.[123]

Rumor has it that Hightower got into an argument with the inspector of the Forest Reserve, Coert DuBois. Whatever the reason for his resignation, Hightower remained in Capitan for many years and at one point was assistant editor for *El Farol*. He ran unsuccessfully for sheriff in 1906 but was appointed U.S. commissioner of the General Land Office in 1908. He established his office in Capitan and was appointed to a second four-year term. In 1914, his wife, Nympha, passed away suddenly on a trip to Socorro. In 1917, he established a homestead just north of Capitan with his daughter, Genevieve, homesteading next to him and taking care of her father and nine-year-old brother in the process. In 1919, Hightower married Lily Romero Jiron and moved to the Hondo Valley, where he was elected to the state legislature in 1926. Hightower drifted about before finally moving to Lower Frisco Plaza, where he passed away in his sleep on August 4, 1931.

BACA RANGER STATION

The Baca Ranger Station was established in 1907, and by October 1911, it had a barn and stock pens. While in existence, the Baca site served the area on the north side of the Capitan Mountains at least as far north as the Block Ranch. A school was located south and a little west from the ranger station across the small arroyo that marked the start of Baca Canyon. At a later time, a sawmill was built on this site sometime before 1867.

Rangers and the dates they were stationed at the Baca Site include Ernest Wright, March 1907–April 1908; John Coleman, May 1908–June 1911; Raymond Rogers, September 1911–March 1913; and Alfred Mullan, March 1913–August 1913. They were followed by Benjamin Nabors, September 1913–August 1916; Rollin Hill, September 1916–April 1917; and Edward Yott, May 1917–August 1917. Next to serve were Frank McLure, August 1917–May 1920; Bernard Hendricks, February 1919–June 1921; W.C. White, July 1921–April 1926; and Vance Thomas, April 1926–January 1927.

Willard Bond was the last ranger at the Baca site from March 1927 until the site closed in August 1929. He says the Capitan office was:

Baca Ranger Station office and dwelling, 1921. *Photograph by O.F. Arthur, FS 152427, courtesy of U.S. Forest Service.*

up there at the old Baca Station, the old Baca ranch headquarters. They called that the Honeymoon Ranger Station. Seems like every Ranger that went there spent their honeymoon there.

It was just an old board station. As I remember, it didn't even have a sink in it. I know it didn't have any plumbing facilities. It had a cistern, and the rats and mice used to get up into it. I wrote to Fred Arthur about that. I told him, "That thing needs a new top on it," and he couldn't understand why I had to have a new cistern top. I told him, "Fred, you come with me and I'll show you." I went out and drew a bucket of water and just threw it on the top, and it just drizzled right on down into the cistern. Fred says, "You win; we'll put a new top on it." And he did.[124]

CAPITAN RANGER STATION

In 1929, the Baca Ranger Station was moved into the village of Capitan, and in 1945, the Gallinas Ranger District was discontinued. Part of the area was moved to the Capitan Ranger District. The first ranger station in Capitan was on Second Street. The second known ranger station was in a house just north of Salado Creek, on the west side of the road, and it was reportedly owned by Hunt Hobbs. The third site was where the Capitan High School football field is today. At present, there is an administrative site in Capitan but no formal office to serve the public.

The Capitan Ranger Station consisted of an office, a residence and a barn. In those days, there were just a couple of United States Forest Service (USFS) personnel, but there were firefighters and watershed project people like Peg Pfingsten and LaMoyne Peters.

Lee Beall was the first ranger at the Capitan site, and he had previously served as ranger at the Nogal Mesa Ranger Station. Beall went from the Mesa to Capitan after they divided the ranger district into the Capitan and Ruidoso Ranger Districts, and he retired out of the Alamogordo office. Richard V. "Dick" Galt followed Beall from the Nogal Mesa into Capitan. After leaving Capitan, he was killed by lightning in the Carlsbad area.

Following Beall and Galt were Ed Pierson, who served from December 1935 to October 1936, and Walter Hackleman, who was stationed in Capitan from December 1936 to March 1945. They were followed by Walter L. Graves, who describes his year and half as ranger of the Capitan District:

> *I was moved to the Capitan District on the Lincoln in the spring of 1945. Earl Moore was supervisor of the Lincoln, and I will say that he was one of the finest supervisors I ever had the privilege of working under. The ranger station at Capitan that we occupied was by far the best facilities that we had ever lived in up to then. It was the show place of the Lincoln, and one of the show places of the region. However, before we left, the house showed evidence of falling apart and, as I understand it, has been falling apart ever since.*
>
> *I well remember that when we left the Long Valley District we had about twenty-six nice laying hens, and since every station we ever occupied had a place for chickens, I brought the chickens to Capitan. When I got there, the supervisor informed me that chickens were not allowed and that I'd have to get rid of them. We kept them in the woodshed for a few weeks, and during that time we killed chickens and ate them just about as fast as we could. Finally, by eating what we could, and canning a few, we were able to get rid of all of our chickens.*
>
> *We were not allowed to keep a horse at the ranger station, so our only alternative was to rent corral space downtown and keep the horse down there. We had no pasture and just kept him in this small corral when he was not being used on the district.*

Ed Guck marking a tree, circa 1950s. *Photograph courtesy of David Cunningham, Smokey Bear State Park.*

While I was at Capitan I had no help except a summer fire guard who was one of the local schoolteachers, and a lookout during fire season, and a small three-man trail crew.[125]

John Humbert served from April 1946 to July 1947; Lawrence Pattison, July 1947 to November 1949; and Dean Earl, November 1949 until August 1951. Earl was the ranger during the Capitan Gap Fire and was the first to let local youth work at the Forest Service. He was especially good at fighting fires. Earl was followed by Paul Wild, who served from September 1951 to July 1954. Wild then went on to Cloudcroft and Alamogordo.

Milton E. "Ed" Guck, also following Beall and Galt from the Nogal Mesa, was the next ranger at the Capitan site, serving from October 1954 to June 1960. The Gucks were at Mayhill before they came to the Nogal Mesa and Capitan and were well respected in the community. Ed covered more country than any other ranger. He would get up in the hills and walk all day long.

Ed Guck's wife, Dorothy, was the sister of previous Mesa site ranger Gordon Gray. Ed Guck was from Brooklyn, and Dorothy Guck had been a classmate of Gerald Ford in Michigan. The couple had three children who lived at the site: Tom, Mick and Mary. Mick and Tom became forest rangers like their father.

Capitan Ranger Station, Lincoln National Forest, circa 1930s. *Photograph courtesy of Garth Hyde.*

In 1960, the Capitan Ranger District became the Smokey Bear Ranger District. Though the name changed, Ed Guck remained the ranger until April 1962. Guck was followed by Ralph Solethers, who served from April 1962 until February 1966, after which he was transferred to the Forest Service headquarters in Washington, D.C. Richard Beaubien served as the ranger from April 1966 to February 1969 before transferring to the Tonto District in Arizona.

Merrill Richards was ranger from May 1969 to July 1969 and was followed by Burt Schulle from August 1969 until September 1970. Thomas Goodrich served from November 1970 until June 1973, when he was transferred to Alamogordo. The last ranger in Capitan was Ronald Daniels, stationed there from June 1973 until December 1973. Daniels had been an assistant ranger under Richard Beaubien and went to Arizona when the Capitan site closed down.

The third Capitan office was built by the WPA in the late 1930s and was located where the high school football field is today. During the time Dick Beaubien was ranger, the office was moved and only the residence was used. Sometime during Tom Goodrich's tenure, the residence was torn down, and a doublewide mobile home was brought in to provide living quarters. The last ranger, Ron Daniels, brought his own mobile home and lived in it until the ranger districts were consolidated in 1974.

On January 1, 1974, the Smokey Bear Ranger District was consolidated with the Ruidoso Ranger District as a part of the Lincoln National Forest.[126]

FOREST SERVICE LOOKOUTS

U.S. Forest Service lookouts were once located throughout Lincoln County. In the 1920s and 1930s, there were ten lookouts in Lincoln County: Monjeau, Ruidoso, Block Ranch, Pine Lodge, Baca, Glencoe, Buck Mountain, Tucson Peak, Patos Mountain and Gavilan Ridge. Only the Ruidoso and Monjeau Lookouts survive.

The Block Lookout on the Block Ranch on the north side of the Capitan Mountains was unique in that it was not a tower but rather a house on the top of a hill surrounded by cottonwoods. From this site, the whole north side of the Capitan Mountains could be viewed. Today, the Forest Service maintains a radio repeater on the site.

Old Block Ranger Station being used as fire guard headquarters, 1921. *Photograph by B.A. Hendricks, FS #161394, courtesy of U.S. Forest Service.*

THE SHOEMAKER INCIDENT[127]

In the early 1920s, Thomas Shoemaker had been in a series of disagreements with the U.S. Forest Service over grazing allotments for cattle, maintaining that the Forest Service was favoring the Block Ranch in allocating grazing allotments. Shoemaker was said to have specifically had trouble with W.C. White, the ranger at the Baca Ranger Station from 1921 to 1926 with jurisdiction over the Capitan Mountains.

In 1926, a forest fire of a suspicious nature started on the north side of the Capitan Mountains. Again, in March 1927, a fire rumored to have been set by Shoemaker started on the north side of the Capitan Mountains. Another story was that cowboys from adjacent ranches set the fire in an attempt to burn Shoemaker out.

Still more stories are related by Shoemaker's granddaughter, Barbara Wagner:

> *We were always told that our grandfather, Mr. Shoemaker, owned a Jersey bull. The tale was that his bull got with some Block Ranch cattle, which angered the cowboys greatly. It seems as though, according to the tale, the cowboys caught the Jersey bull and castrated it and it consequently died…*
>
> *Another thing that I seem to recall is that my grandfather was burning weeds out of a tank and the fire got away from him and the result was that the fire did burn a part of the forest…*[128]

He was reportedly seen at the fire where he even talked to the fire crews, mostly asking questions pertaining to fighting the fire. Local legend says that rangers followed Shoemaker back to his corral, where he put his horse up and went into his house.

Firefighters were brought in from as far off as the Nogal Mesa Ranger Station. One of them was Herbert Lee Traylor, who at the time was attending high school in the village of Lincoln. He states that he was picked up by a truck driven by Barney Luck Sr. and dropped off in the area of the Block Ranch, where it "appeared that the whole North Side of the Capitans was on fire, and the smoke was blowing to the east for many miles."

Firefighters were placed south of where the fire started and began working to the northeast making firebreaks of areas where the fire had not burned. The wind was blowing with twenty- to thirty-mile gusts, and the firefighters were told if the fire jumped their line not to "go to the ground" but to head west toward the old burn. Men on horses supplied food and water, and the fire was eventually under control. The men began mop-up work, and in doing so, they were told to immediately report the presence of anyone riding in the area who was not part of the firefighting crew.

On the evening of March 15, a firefighter unloading tools from his vehicle near Shoemaker's ranch was shot at, supposedly by T.H. Shoemaker. J.A. Brubaker, a former forest ranger living in Capitan, called Fred Arthur, the Lincoln National Forest supervisor whose office was located in Alamogordo, to report the incident and indicated that evidence had been collected associating Shoemaker with the fire. Mr. Arthur, in turn, called a Mr. French, assistant solicitor in Albuquerque, requesting that he come and investigate the incident.

From the Coalora Coal Mines to Smokey Bear

Arthur arrived at Capitan at 5:00 p.m. with executive assistant W.C. White. White had been a forest ranger in the Capitan District and was brought along to keep records dealing with the fire. Arthur and White were given an update on the situation.

When the fire started, Ranger Willard Bond left the Baca Ranger Station with A.R. Dean and Dean's son-in-law, Lloyd Taylor, the foreman of the Block Ranch where the fire was. They carried chuck and fire boxes with them. Bond had a rifle, and Dean had a pistol that he picked up in Capitan on the way. Traveling in Dean's car, they met Ranger Lee Beall and other men.

They left the highway near the fire and stopped at a closed gate directly in front of T.H. Shoemaker's house. At that point, they left their cars to fight the fire. About 2:00 a.m. Ranger Bond moved Beall's car two miles to the east to the fire camp. At sunrise, Lloyd Taylor, Charles Pepper and Apolinario Romero returned to the remaining car for supplies. Pepper carried a lantern and was standing at the rear of the car as Taylor was getting supplies from the front seat when two shots were fired at them from the Shoemaker house. Pepper, hit in the back of the neck by a rock fragment, put out the lantern. All three men took cover, and Taylor eventually got the equipment needed to fight the fire.

Assistant Solicitor French arrived from Albuquerque at 11:00 p.m., and he and Arthur left for the fire about 5:00 a.m. on the seventeenth. Upon arriving at the scene, they went over the fire lines and interviewed those involved in the shooting but discovered that there was not enough evidence to establish the identity of the shooter. They also learned that Bond's and Dean's weapons had been stolen from Dean's car when they moved it to the fire camp. Upon closer inspection, it was discovered that the shots fired at Pepper and Taylor both hit the car, one entering the right front of the car and passing through the rear cushions and the second hitting the running board and damaging the wiring on the underside of the car. Both shots had barely missed Lloyd Taylor.

Charley Pepper was approached, but he refused to file a complaint, and Apolinario Romero did not press changes. Lloyd Taylor had returned to the Block Ranch to repair a windmill and would not return for several days. Ranger Willard Bond stated that he was anxious to get his rifle back and would file a complaint with the county sheriff. The group drove to Carrizozo, where Bond filed his complaint with Sheriff Sam Kelsey, and a search warrant was obtained, to be served by Kelsey the next day.

Just as the Arthur party was leaving Carrizozo, they received a call from A.R. Dean telling them that he, along with Lloyd Taylor and Charley Pepper, was coming into Carrizozo to see the sheriff, and he asked Arthur not to leave. When Dean returned to the camp from fighting the fire, he noticed the damage to his vehicle from the rifle shots. Taylor arrived unexpectedly from repairing the windmill, and the three men decided to file a complaint against Shoemaker. This was discussed with justice of the peace A.H. Harvey and Sheriff Kelsey, while Taylor discussed the situation with Truman A. Spencer Sr., who managed the Block Ranch. The Block Ranch had received many threats from Shoemaker, culminating with shots fired at Taylor the previous day. Complaints were sworn out for assault with a deadly weapon, and Sheriff Kelsey told the group he would be in Capitan the next morning at 8:00 a.m. and would need the assistance of Forest Service personnel.

The plan was for Kelsey and Dean to go to the Dixon Ranch on the opposite side of the mountain from Shoemaker and to ask Dixon (who was friendly with Shoemaker) to talk Shoemaker into surrendering. Lloyd Taylor and Newt Kemp would be at the Hipp Ranch one mile north of Shoemaker's ranch. Deputy Sheriff Pete Johnson and one Forest Service authority would be at the Koprian Ranch. Ranger Arthur was deputized as a Lincoln County sheriff. Finally, a deputy sheriff was to be stationed at the fire camp to coordinate movements. If Dixon refused to participate or Shoemaker refused to surrender, Kelsey and Dean were to return and make the arrest. If any of the groups were to come across Shoemaker, they were to arrest him immediately.

The previous night, Ranger Bond had returned to the fire camp and directed Strickland to have two men watch Shoemaker's ranch. After watching the house from a distance, Strickland and White returned and reported that Shoemaker was in his house. The official Forest Service report has Deputy Sheriff Pete Johnson, Arthur and White driving to the Koprian Ranch in a Forest Service pickup truck with White driving and Johnson in the front seat. Arthur sat on a spare tire in the back. All three had rifles.[129]

When White reached the highway, he turned west toward Encinoso, driving about a mile and a half before they came upon two horses with a female rider on the road to Shoemaker's ranch.[130] Driving past the horses, Arthur saw Shoemaker standing at the rear of one of the horses with his hand near the butt of a rifle. White stopped about 100 to 150 yards past the road when Johnson got out and started walking back to where the horses and people were standing. Johnson supposedly said, "Mr. Shoemaker, we want to talk to you." Shoemaker reached for his weapon, and Johnson, unarmed, turned and came back to the truck, saying, "Look out, he is going to shoot." Arthur grabbed his gun and went to the front of the car while White sat in the driver's seat.

Shoemaker started shooting, and Arthur returned fire. It is said that Shoemaker's first shot hit White in the back of the head. Johnson got back to the vehicle and grabbed his rifle before kneeling at the right front of the car, at the same time blocking Arthur's line of fire. Shoemaker and Johnson kept firing at each other, but Arthur was limited to firing underneath the vehicle. During the exchange of gunfire, Arthur saw White slip down but thought he was trying to get out of the gunfire. He next saw White slide out of the car and pitch face forward into a rut.

The woman on the horse had moved away from the shooting and was watching the event from the north side of the road. After the second or third shot, Shoemaker's horse was hit and fell down. The firing stopped, and Arthur saw Shoemaker lying on the ground. Arthur went to White, and Johnson started toward Shoemaker when Shoemaker started crawling toward his rifle. Johnson ran back, got more bullets from Arthur and shot Shoemaker for a final time. One of the horses was badly wounded, and Johnson shot it, too.

Barbara Wagner, a direct descendant of Shoemaker's, writes:

> *Along about this time the Feds and Mr. Shoemaker were in a disagreement about the measurement of land included in the homestead. In the homestead earlier we understood it would be okay. Then he built a water tank for his livestock and he had it included in the homestead. Later, the Federal Rangers began fencing it out into Forest land. He would redo the fence including his tank, this led to his being accused of setting forest fires…The bitter mess between the rangers and Mr. Shoemaker intensified. Other people felt in jeopardy as they became aware of the situation. Many were packing guns and discussions were occurring. One morning he rode his horse down to the mailbox and when the mail car arrived, a pregnant woman jumped out of the car warning him "Mr. Shoemaker, they have come to kill you." The men jumped out of the car, Pete Johnson and another man. They started firing; Mr. Shoemaker couldn't get his rifle out of the saddle scabbard and was firing from that position. Evidently he was on the horse and was shot as was the horse. As he lay dying, Pete Johnson walked over and shot Mr. Shoemaker in the head.*[131]

Pete Mocho, Shoemaker's grandson, tells a similar story but with different details:

> *Mother's father was killed over a line dispute in the mid 1920s. I do not know the details…My grandfather was an avid sportsman. He loved to*

hunt. He never left the house without his gun. The day he was killed, he left the house with his shotgun to walk down to the mailbox to pick up the mail. He met a Mr. White at the mailbox where, apparently an argument occurred and he was shot by Mr. White, who claimed self-defense, pointing to grandfather's gun. There were no other witnesses so the whole story cannot be told.[132]

White was shot in the face and mortally wounded. Johnson wanted to take him to the Fort Stanton hospital, but a bullet had penetrated the radiator and the car would not go more than a mile. Arthur left Johnson with White and went to the fire camp. When he returned, Johnson had taken White to Fort Stanton on the mail truck, but White died. The woman on the horse was the wife of Guy Nix, a Block Ranch cowboy.

Word was sent to Ranger Lee Beall in Capitan to send a truck to tow the Forest Service vehicle back to town. Herbert Lee Traylor was asked to go with J.P. Haley to drive the three-quarter-ton Dodge Forest Service truck back to town with the disabled vehicle in tow. They arrived at the site of the killing about 2:00 p.m. and found the following scene:

A dead horse lay across the road behind the pickup truck that had been shot up. Mr. Shoemaker was laying on his back about three steps toward the road from the mailbox. An old coat covered his chest and head. I recall that he had on brogan shoes—without spurs, dark trousers, a plaid shirt, and a blue denim jumper.

The car the Forest Service officials had been in at the time of the fracas was in the main road, slightly west of the mailbox. Cars had been detouring around it on the left side.[133]

The damaged truck was hitched to the one sent from Capitan. Shoemaker's body was placed in the first truck, and Traylor was instructed to tow the damaged truck to Brubaker's Garage in Capitan, where a hearse would meet them to take the body to Carrizozo. A coroner's inquest was held over Shoemaker's body, including testimony by Mrs. Nix, and a search was made of his house, where the missing weapons were found. Thomas Shoemaker was buried in Carrizozo.

Herbert Lee Traylor probably summed it up fairly when he wrote:

The "Old Gentleman" undoubtedly did not intend to hurt anyone other than the Forest Rangers, and probably he was particularly after White.

If he had shot the Sheriff as he ran back to the pickup truck he might very well have killed all four of them. However, he was probably intent on shooting White and had no quarrel with Pete [Johnson].

You will remember the fire I am talking about was in 1927 and there had been one in the same area also in 1926. The best I can find out there were only small lighting fires from the time I am talking about until the "Great Smokey Bear Fire" in 1950, which we know was caused by a sawmill. Whether the "Old Gentleman" caused the fires in the twenties will never be proven. I leave it to you for your consideration.[134]

CIVILIAN CONSERVATION CORPS AND NATIONAL YOUTH ADMINISTRATION CAMPS

There were nine listed Federal Civilian Conservation Corps (CCC) camps in Lincoln County. The Baca Campsite sits in the southern foothills of the Capitan Mountains, on the site of the former Hispanic settlement Baca Camp. The site was also the home of the Capitan Ranger Station, and a CCC Camp, Camp Capitan DF-17-N, was located here in 1933–35. The men's CCC camp was abandoned by 1935. Another camp for girls, Camp Capitan, one of the few in the United States, was located also at this site from 1935 to 1940.

Changed from a camp for men, Camp Capitan transitioned to women in 1935 as a program of the National Youth Association (NYA) and the Works Project Administration (WPA). The camp consisted of a large log dining hall, kitchen and storeroom, six barracks, an infirmary and a cottage built around a patio surrounded by pines.

Mr. and Mrs. A.K. Shaw were appointed to organize a camp for girls in New Mexico in September 1935, with Lucy Shaw as the director of the camp and A.K. acting as the superintendent of maintenance. With no funding available, WPA cleaned it up, and furniture was obtained from other state agencies. The WPA sewing program in Capitan provided the sheets, pillowcases and blankets. Utensils for the kitchens were provided from various sources in the area, and Fort Stanton provided two stoves. Fort Bayard supplied furniture, rugs and mirrors. When the camp opened, there were two hundred beds ready for the young women.

Upon arrival, the girls had health examinations by doctors from Fort Stanton, followed by informal instruction in English, social science, mathematics, history and stenography. All participants also received instruction in household management, meal planning, cooking, food value and serving. Among the first instructors were Ruth Penfield, Lou Fink, Virginia Brown, Jane McLane, Claudia Pacheco and Margery Wilson.

Later attendees were reduced to 125 girls, who were paid five dollars a month, plus twenty-five dollars sent home to their parents. The sewing classes made garments for the Tingley Hospital for Crippled Children, while New Mexico state flags were made for every school. Additionally, tinware was made for the White Sands National Monument.

Traditional Spanish arts of colcha embroidery, weaving, wool spinning, curing and drying of hides and the making of jackets and moccasins were taught. Other skills included woodworking, linoleum printing and painting, as well as instruction in musical arts and plays. The walls of the recreation building, better known as the Baca Canyon Opera House, were covered by murals painted by the girls.

At the end of each three-month term, an open house was held for the local communities, featuring plays and light operas, sewing, woven rugs and blankets and tinware made by the girls. In 1938, the *Lincoln County News* described one such open house, saying, "All the girls seemed happy and buoyant. The Spanish girls were especially striking in their dark beauty, wearing white blouses gathered to full square yokes which were covered with vivid colcha embroidery, and having very full gathered sleeves trimmed the same way."[135]

That presentation concluded with a presentation of *The Mikado*, by Gilbert and Sullivan, performed in Spanish rhythm. Credit was given to Rosemary Quinn, the music instructor, and Mrs. Pacheco, Freda Burton and Barbara Reeves, the costume directors.

Activities included folk dancing, ballroom dancing, quilting, baseball, basketball, croquet, badminton, hiking and volleyball. A newspaper, the *Mountain Echo*, was published every two weeks. Dances were also sponsored with the boys from local CCC camps, chaperoned by the barracks mothers and with music provided by the Lou Fink Orchestra, composed of boys from the Carrizozo CCC camp.

Rita Sanchez Roybal, the daughter of Ramoncita Gurule, best summed up her mother's experience at Camp Capitan:

> *Our beloved mother was a young girl at Camp Capitan. What memories you brought back of the young years our younger sister and I shared with her! She had a big, black trunk and a cedar chest full of stuff—some of the things she made at Camp Capitan. She had a cookbook with hand written recipes. She taught us to embroider and crochet. She made us dresses from colorful flower sacks. We would go to Vidaurri Grocery Store and pick out the flour sack*

National Youth Administration women's site at Camp Capitan, circa 1938. *Photograph courtesy of Eddie Womack.*

> *design that would later become matching dresses for my sister, Rosylene and I. She decorated the dresses with rickrack trim. They were beautiful! I'm so glad she attended Camp Capitan. She learned to be creative.*[136]

Was the camp successful? Perhaps the *Lincoln County News* summed it up best in 1938: "Over a period of three years, we heard the government's Educational Camp for Girls, National Youth Administration project, discussed from many angles—praised by some, criticized by others and spoken indifferently by the majority."[137]

The camp was closed in 1940 due to lack of funds. At the start of World War II, this camp became the site for Japanese railroad workers from Clovis who were interned at the beginning of the war.[138]

Raton Ranch

The general area around the Baca Campsite and CCC camp was also known as Raton Ranch. Situated fifteen miles northeast of Capitan, the camp sat six thousand feet above sea level, on an almost impassible dirt road in a grove of trees.

With the coming of World War II, December 1941 found a group of immigrant railroad workers from Japan living in Clovis and working on the railroad. It was decided that these families needed to be moved for their own good, and Raton Ranch was selected. The former CCC camp (F-17-N) fit the bill because it was isolated and already established. The Japanese left Clovis at midnight on January 24, and they arrived at Raton Ranch (Baca Campsite) at 7:00 a.m. The camp was reached by twelve miles of bad road that tore up cars and made communication and supply difficult.[139]

Detained in the camp were thirty Japanese, seventeen of whom were Japanese-American citizens, with the oldest only twenty-one years old. P.W. Herrick of the U.S. State Department described the camp. The internees were former workers from the Santa Fe Railroad in Clovis, who had been

> removed to Raton for their own protection, since their safety had been threatened at that town. Detainment orders had been taken out against them so that they could be detained for their own protection. However, no case had been built up against them. This camp is more a place of refuge for persons threatened with mob violence than a detention camp.[140]
>
> The camp is surrounded by a barbed wire fence, which is not guarded, and upon arriving at the camp the gates to the one entrance were opened by one of the detainees. Two border patrol officers live within the enclosure of the camp with their wives. These are the only authorities at the camp.
>
> The camp consists of five or six buildings that were erected a number of years ago by the CCC. In three of these, the detainees are quartered in family groups. The other buildings include living quarters for the border patrol officers and their wives, a food warehouse and office and camp headquarters. All these buildings are built of wood covered with tar paper.[141]

Food for the camp was supplied by the border patrol and was cooked and eaten in family groups. When detainees became ill, their own families treated them, and the more serious cases were taken to the merchant marine hospital at Fort Stanton. The detainees were allowed to send and receive mail without censorship. Radios were allowed but not short wave-radios. For recreation, the detainees walked around the camp, played games or planted small gardens and shrubs and improved the landscaping around the camp.[142]

Shiro Ebihara wrote to a railroad official in Clovis in June 1942:

Everyone is just fine here in this camp. The garden consisting of different kinds of vegetables are coming up just fine. Also the flowers are starting to bloom and I'm sure this camp's surroundings will be beautiful soon.... Again I want to thank you for doing so much for each of us. I hope to be able to return someday when all this confusion clears up. [143]

The internees suffered due to the isolation and being required to remain indoors due to the weather. The children initially went to the public school in Capitan but were withdrawn after hostility in the community. Opal Miles, wife of Governor John Miles, eventually got involved, but the Lincoln County Board of Education rebuffed all efforts to put the children in local schools. Amy Ebihara, formerly a junior at Clovis High School, became the teacher for the internees using books donated from Clovis. [144]

On August 19, 1942, Mr. Franciso de Amat, Spanish consul at San Francisco, and Mr. Sanz, assistant to the Spanish consul, made an inspection of the Civilian Detention Center at Raton Ranch. They were accompanied on the trip by Mr. P.W. Herrick of the U.S. Department of State. In charge of the camp were Inspector William C. Wright and Inspector Griffin, officers of the border patrol, Immigration and Naturalization Service. The internees were represented by Miss Ebihara.

The Spanish inspectors were impressed with the camp, which resembled a small country community rather than a detention camp. The detainees had unlimited freedom in the camp, and the border patrol officers and their wives took an interest in the detainees. The only complaint was from a Mr. Nakashima, who requested to be reunited with his family interned in Tulare, California. He requested that his family be transferred to Raton Ranch, and if that were not possible, that he be transferred to Tulare. [145]

Camp officials eventually realized that the camp presented too many problems, and the internees were transferred in December 1942 to War Relocation Authority (WRA) camps in Utah and Arizona.

CHAPTER 8

SMOKEY BEAR

Smokey the Bear, Smokey the Bear
Huffing and puffing and sniffing the air
—"Smokey the Bear"
Lyrics by Steve Nelson and Jack Rollins

Fires are unavoidable in mountain forests, and Lincoln County is no exception. Almost every year, there is a wildland fire, sometimes caused by a natural event, such as a lightning strike, but most often these fires are man-made. Some years are dryer than others, and this magnifies the intensity and number of fires. The Forest Service, Bureau of Land Management, State Forestry and local fire departments are organized and trained to fight these fires. Significant fires have occurred in 1926, 1927 (Shoemaker Fire), 1994 (Pancho Fire) and 2004 (Peppin Fire).

Regardless of the time, size and cause of the fire, these wildland firefighters are dedicated and quick to respond when called, as they have been for over one hundred years. While there are fires almost every year, one in 1950 was especially significant.

SAWMILLS ON THE CAPITANS

The first recorded mention of a sawmill in the Capitan Mountains was in 1900. There was a sawmill on the northern edge of West Mountain whose operator's name was probably Gumm. Every day he would take a team of mules down the north side of the mountain to fill tanks of water at the Lon Merchant Ranch and then take them back up the mountain to the mill.[146]

From the 1930s to the 1950s, the Upper Hondo Water District had contracts to cut and mill logs on the mountains, and the people operating the sawmill had built a road up on the mountain. Willis Whitcamp operated a chain of those sawmills along the base of the north side of the Capitan Mountains. The Forest Service would have Whitcamp and his sawmill crew logs in the canyons wherever the beetles were bad. They would cut underbrush in the winter due to the snow and inclement weather and log seasonally when weather permitted. They would move their cabin on skids into the canyons and stay for several years until the logging was completed in that area.[147]

In May 1950, there was a sawmill midway down the north side of Capitan Mountain at the mouth of Las Tablas Canyon. Willis Whitcamp resided in a cabin there with at least five workers.

LAS TABLAS FIRE

The first of two fires began on Thursday, May 4, 1950, when a cook stove at the Whitcamp sawmill overheated and cast sparks, resulting in a fire that would take two days to contain. The fire was particularly intense on Capitan Mountain. Fanned by winds of up to seventy miles per hour, Whitcamp drove to the Merchant Ranch and requested help from the Forest Service. The Las Tablas Fire burned approximately one thousand acres before fire crews had it under control on May 6, two days later.

Firefighters came to the Whitcamp sawmill and said they would be able to stop the fire, but later mounted horsemen came back and said to vacate; the fire had jumped the gap. Whitcamp and his people buried all their tools and sawmill equipment in an effort to keep it from burning. They also turned all of their mules and horses loose. When they returned after the fire, they found the only thing that had burned was the carriage that they had not covered with dirt.[148]

By the next morning, the fire had completely burned the Whitcamp site, and a call was sent out for help, including to Fort Bliss near El Paso. Local ranchers and residents of Capitan reported to the rapidly growing base camp on the north side of the Capitan Gap. Game Warden Ray Bell had

Dean Earl and Ray Bell in Capitan Gap after the fire on May 11, 1950. Note the sign pointing to Whitcamp Sawmill. *U.S. Forest Service photograph by Harold Walker courtesy of David Cunningham, Smokey Bear State Park.*

landed his Piper aircraft in an open pasture and soon took Dean Earl aloft to survey the damage. The flight lasted about thirty minutes while Earl mapped the fire and its course.

Due to the quick action of the firefighters, the fire was declared secure on Saturday, May 6 at 2:30 p.m. Some firefighters were kept on the fire line to mop up, but most were sent home, and the breaking down of the base camp began.[149]

Paul Jones, is the son of homesteaders in the area, and he has spent a lifetime working in the Lincoln National Forest. He remembers:

> *Dean Earl was the ranger. Ed Guck was sent into the ranger station and served as a dispatcher. Ray Bell had access to the Game Department plane and used it to observe fires. This was the first time they used a plane on the Lincoln. The sawmill was towards the base of the mountain on the north side. A stove blew over, and sparks got out in Las Tablas Canyon. They pretty well got that under control and released people working on fire. The*

theory is that they released people, and one of them started a fire in the gap.
It went both east and west.[150]

Doyle Cozzens, then a high school student, was part of the firefighting effort:

When the first fire started, the Forest Service had regular people to fight it,
including high school kids. After a couple of days we had it under control. One
of the nights we were working the trails we ran across a burnt bear in a tree, but
Jim McEuen, our crew chief, would not have anything to do with it.[151]

THE CAPITAN GAP FIRE

The second fire started on May 6 and was also believed to have been started by humans. It is suspected the fire was caused by a tossed cigarette or purposely set by a dismissed firefighter. Upon seeing the new smoke in the Capitan Gap, those striking the base camp headed to the scene. Again with the wind blowing very hard and having to cover over a mile of rough road to get to what would become known as the Capitan Gap Fire, crews were in a race against time. It would prove to be a race they would lose. Lee Beall recalled, "In a short eight or ten hours, the whole side of the mountain burned off."[152]

Hollis Cummins was taken to the south of the gap by Lincoln County sheriff Sally Ortiz to watch for other fires while the Las Tablas Fire was burning. When there, the Capitan Gap Fire started, and Ortiz came and got him. They stopped while going through the gap to try to put up a fire line, but the fire crowned in the trees and branched in both directions. The fire to the west stopped, but the one to the east continued to burn. One group of firefighters was caught on rocks by the fire, and members had to carry a man out with them.[153]

Soon, the fire grew to such proportions that the base camp had to be evacuated. Wally Ferguson, another high school student at the time of the fire, remembers:

I was fourteen, and my dad took me with him on the pumper truck, and
we were riding around spraying stumps. They had a big camp where Gap
Road met Base Road. A forest ranger came and told us a big fire started
in the gap and to take the pumper up there. My dad, G.W. Chapman, Bill
Randle and I went up in the gap, and a fire was roaring toward Little
Mountain and the fire was getting hot. Sam Service built a backfire along
road. Trees started on fire on the east side of road, and it got out of control.

Bill Randale said to cover up heads and jumped a wash out. When we went by the base camp it was abandoned and burned through.[154]

The base camp was reestablished to the north where the Capitan Gap road met Highway 246 and would eventually support over five hundred people. Initially, food was in short supply, and Capitan housewives sent sandwiches to the firefighters. Later, many of the supplies came from the Murphy and Titsworth Stores in Capitan.

One of the people at the base camp was Dorothy Guck, wife of Ranger Ed Guck. In her travels around Arizona and New Mexico as a ranger's wife, Dorothy began writing for local newspapers. Ironically, she would be the only reporter covering the Capitan Gap Fire and would call in her stories to the *Lincoln County News* on a daily basis.

Doyle Cozzens continues describing his participation in fighting the fire:

We got the fire under control, and Jim McEuen was driving us back to town on a Sunday afternoon. A new fire had started right in the gap. Jim

Dean Earl and Ray Bell observe devastation of the Capitan Gap Fire, May 11, 1950. *U.S. Forest Service Photograph by Harold Walker courtesy of David Cunningham, Smokey Bear State Park.*

stopped the truck with flames all around and said, "If the gas tank catches on fire, let me know." They called us back that night or the next day. The best I can remember, we only went out one time when they requested the army from Fort Bliss. The fire was totally out of control.

They hired a heavy equipment operator from the county, Henry Morgan, to come out and supervise a crew. That next night the crew we were on got trapped by the fire and we had to go sideways on a rockslide to avoid fire on east mountain. After that, all the high school kids were limited to working in the camps—making sandwiches and headlamps, etc.

Not long after that, a soldier from Fort Bliss came in with a bear cub tucked in his jacket he found on east mountain side.[155]

Eventually, the Capitan Gap Fire grew to over seventeen thousand acres. The fire was contained on May 9, and when a group of firefighters looked up, they saw a small black bear cub clinging to a tree with its mother nowhere in sight. The cub's paws were severely burned, and it was terrified and near death from shock, burns and hunger. Briefly named "Hotfoot Teddy," he was about to take his place in history as the living symbol "Smokey Bear."

SMOKEY BEAR

Six years before the fire, a fictional bear was designated as the fire prevention symbol of the nation. Because of concern that fires would destroy vital national resources during World War II, the Wartime Advertising Council and the National Smokey Fire Prevention Campaign distributed posters of a bear wearing coveralls and a ranger's hat telling the public of the dangers of forest fires.

Early on the morning of May 8, a group of soldiers who came to help fight the fire were awaiting relief when a young bear cub came toward them and then climbed a tree. The soldiers watched the cub for about twenty minutes before being relieved and moving on. The cub followed them briefly before it disappeared.

That same morning, Lee "Speed" Simmons led another group of soldiers to the top of Capitan Mountain to try and build a fire line to contain the fire before winds got up later in the day. The fire got out of control to the group's rear, and they had to run to a rockslide area to avoid being overcome. Reaching the rocks with about two minutes to spare, they hunkered down, and all survived due to Simmons's leadership.

It is probable that the young bear cub had followed the same course as Simmons and his party and had gone to the rocks. When the fire had passed, he climbed up a tree. Unlike the humans, the cub was badly burned, but luckily for him, the soldiers looked up and saw him.

The tiny bear cub was brought back to the fire camp. Crew leaders were Ross Flatley and Ernest Purcella. G.W. Chapman was also in the crew that found the cub clinging to a tree. The group reached the base camp about 5:00 p.m. on May 9 with the cub in tow.

Once the bear was brought into camp, Ross Flatley took it home in an empty food box, where he and his wife, Patricia, nursed him through the first night, despite the bear's wailing. Flatley was later heard to say he should have knocked the bear in the head when he got him.[156]

New Mexico game warden Ray Bell, who had been flying over the fire for fire boss Dean Earl, had heard of the burned cub. Bell knew the cub needed medical attention, and the best veterinarian he knew was in Santa Fe. Bell loaded the little cub in the airplane the next day and flew him to Santa Fe.

Ruth Bell with Smokey Bear, May 1950. *U.S. Forest Service photograph by Harold Walker, courtesy of David Cunningham, Smokey Bear State Park.*

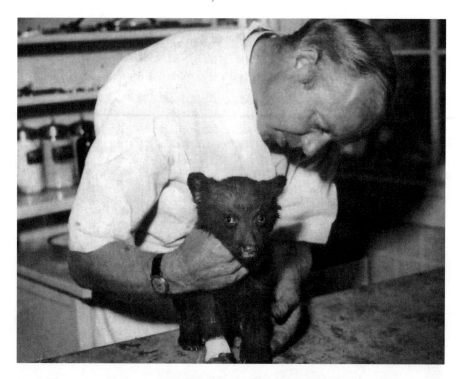

Smokey Bear being treated by Dr. Edwin Smith in Santa Fe, May 1950. *U.S. Forest Service photograph by Patt Meara, courtesy of David Cunningham, Smokey Bear State Park.*

In Santa Fe, veterinarian Edwin Smith first checked the bear's paws and found the equivalent to second-degree burns on the right one. Smith next treated Smokey's backside and stomach. There were no swollen lymph glands to signal infection, and his teeth and eyes were normal. Satisfied, Smith finished his forty-five-minute exam and returned the bear to Bell. Smith estimated Smokey's age at two and a half months. He later predicted that if the cub did not succumb to infection, he would probably survive his burns.[157]

Once well on the way to recovery, Bell took Smokey home, where his wife, Ruth, and daughter Judy helped to nurse the cub back to health for the next month and a half. Bell suggested this cub become the living symbol of fire prevention in the Forest Service's Smokey Bear campaign to chief game warden Elliott Barker, who liked the idea. Barker visited Kester "Kay" Flock, supervisor of the Santa Fe National Forest. Flock contacted the Forest Service in Washington, D.C., and they also liked the idea. A decision was made to take Smokey to Washington and put him in the National Zoo as the living symbol of fire prevention.

Five-year-old Judy Bell with Smokey Bear, May 1950. *U.S. Forest Service photograph by Harold Walker, courtesy of David Cunningham, Smokey Bear State Park.*

On June 27, 1950, pilot Frank Hines of Hobbs, New Mexico, deputy game warden Homer Pickens and Kay Flock left Santa Fe to deliver Smokey to the National Zoo. At that time, the bear cub was about three months old and weighed ten pounds. The Piper cub aircraft was met by enthusiastic crowds at each stop along the way. The plane landed at Washington and taxied to the Presidential Suite. At 11:00 a.m. on June 30, the State of New Mexico and the U.S. Forest Service officially presented the small bear cub to the National Zoo.

Life in Washington was good for Smokey as he matured. More than four million people visited Smokey annually at the National Zoo, and the bear received so much mail that he was assigned his own zip code (20252). Forest Service artists humanized Smokey in posters by portraying him in a stiff-

Above: Ray Bell watches Smokey Bear walk on the plane he flew Smokey in from Capitan to Santa Fe on May 10, 1950. *U.S. Forest Service photograph by Harold Walker, courtesy of David Cunningham, Smokey Bear State Park.*

Below: Homer Pickens and Smokey Bear pose by a Will Schuster painting of Smokey Bear on an airplane before flying to Washington, D.C. on June 27, 1950. *U.S. Forest Service photograph by Harold Walker, courtesy of David Cunningham, Smokey Bear State Park.*

Smokey Bear at the National Zoo, circa 1960s. *Photograph courtesy of David Cunningham, Smokey Bear State Park.*

brimmed campaign cover and with a quizzical look on his face. In 1952, the Junior Forest Ranger Program was established. Also in 1952, the Smokey Bear song was written by Steve Nelson and Jack Rollins, and soon the whole nation was singing it. Throughout his life, Smokey associated with other bears. Goldie, a female bear, was brought to the zoo in an effort to produce offspring, but this was unsuccessful.

THE DEATH OF SMOKEY BEAR

As Smokey aged and it became apparent that he would soon die, the Forest Service decided to return him to Capitan for burial at the new state park named for him. Developing and implementing that plan fell to the fire resource officer of the Lincoln National Forest, Dick Cox, who had recently transferred into that position. Cox was a fifth-generation descendant of early Lincoln County settlers. He had watched the Capitan Gap Fire in May 1950 from the steps of Capitan High School with his future wife, Donna Cloud.

Smokey passed away on November 9, 1976, in Washington at the age of twenty-six. He was packed in dry ice and taken to the TWA office at National Airport and loaded onto TWA Flight 217 departing at 2:00 pm. The plane landed at Albuquerque at 6:30 p.m.

The call came in to Cox about 8:00 a.m., but the plan had been changed because somewhere in the process of planning for the burial, a rumor started that unknown people were going to steal the bear's body en route and cut off his paws.

Paul Jones and Jim Paxton drove a four-by-four truck to put the bear's body in, while Ray Page and Bob Wagenfehr followed in another vehicle. Upon arrival at Albuquerque, they drove right onto the tarmac and loaded Smokey on the truck while being observed by two television crews and a reporter. About ten Forest Service personnel were also there, and the loading only took about five minutes. The small convoy was escorted the whole way back to Capitan by the New Mexico State Police driving in relays.

Back in Capitan, the grave was not dug until after dark for security. The little convoy arrived at the Smokey Bear State Park about 9:00 p.m. The grave was surrounded by four or five cars with the participants using the headlights for illumination. Among the participants were state policeman Jack Johnson and his wife, Marguerite "Chuck," who had brought straps to lower the box into the ground. Two deer hunters had noticed the commotion, and they wandered over to see what was happening.

About eight or ten people, including the two Texans, who were staying in Capitan while hunting deer, lowered the box into the ground, and a backhoe covered it up. Pictures were taken, and the backhoe was parked over the grave for the night. Reporters from a television station showed up about 10:00 p.m. and were skeptical about the burial. They were told they would just have to take the Forest Service's word for it.[158]

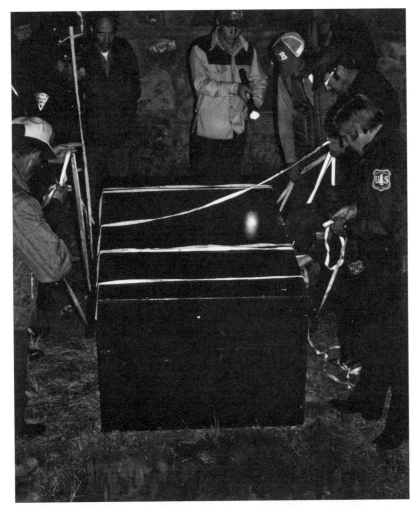

Burial of Smokey Bear on November 9, 1976. The people in this photograph are unidentified, but those who were present include Dick Cox, Paul Jones, Ray Page, Bob Wagenfehr, Steve McCowsky, Jim Abbott and Larry Allen, all of the Forest Service; New Mexico state policeman Jack Johnson and his wife, Marguerite (Chuck); Jay Johnston, mayor of Capitan, and Ray Provine; and two deer hunters from Texas. *Photograph by Larry Allen, courtesy of David Cunningham, Smokey Bear State Park.*

Paul Jones, the assistant fire officer of the Lincoln National Forest staff, participated in the burial and relates:

> They flew him from Washington, D.C., into Albuquerque. Ray Page (district ranger) Jim Paxton, Bob Wagenfehr and myself went to pick him up and had two vehicles and had police escort. State Policeman Jack Johnson met us at San Antonio and our speed stressed out the old Forest Service vehicles. There was a rumor that a group was going to hijack the bear and hijack the paws. We got to Capitan after dark and buried him. They had a little group—the mayor was Jay Johnson, and he had a backhoe and the grave dug when we got there. We lowered it over the grave and it was rearranged later.[159]

Dick Cox writes:

> I buried Smokey. We had a plan, an elaborate one, and one morning I got to work and they told me Smokey had died. I came to Capitan and made sure the grave was dug. Ray Provine worked for village and dug the grave with backhoe. Paul Jones, Bob Page and Ray Wagenfehr met the plane in Albuquerque. The group got there after dark during hunting deer season. Hunters from Texas came out of a bar across from Smokey Bear Restaurant and helped us lower the green box in the ground. Ray Provine parked his backhoe on top of the grave. The rumor was someone was going to steal the claws off of the bear.[160]

Before the bear's death, Ray Page, Smokey Bear Ranger District ranger, and Capitan mayor Jay Johnston drove out to the area where Smokey was found in search of a boulder to mark his grave. They found a one-thousand-pound polished granite boulder near the road and took it back to Capitan, where it was placed over the bear's grave. The plaque on Smokey's grave reads:

> This is the final resting place of the first living Smokey Bear. In 1950 when Smokey was a tiny cub, wildfire burned his forest home in the nearby Capitan Mountains of the Lincoln National Forest. Firefighters found the badly burned cub clinging to a blackened tree and saved his life. In June 1950, the cub was flown to our Nation's Capitol to become the living symbol of wildfire prevention and wildlife conservation. After 25 years he was replaced by another orphaned black bear from the Lincoln National Forest.

SMOKEY BEAR MUSEUM

In 1955, the Capitan Women's Club raised money to place signs to the east and west of town proclaiming Capitan to be the "Home of Smokey Bear." Dorothy Guck chaired the dedication ceremony.

Three years later, in 1958, Mrs. Guck began developing plans to build a Smokey Bear Museum in Capitan. With the Women's Club providing support, Margaret Rench and Pearl Soderback were the driving force behind the fundraising for the museum. The bulk of the donations for the museum came from dances at the American Legion Hall sponsored by Joe and Margaret Rench. Capitan residents also raised money through bake sales and other fundraisers.

Land for the monument was donated by Bill and Adelaide Holmes and Hollis Cummins. Logs from trees cut on Capitan Mountain were marked by Ed Guck and transported into town by J.G. and Herman Otero and Trankie Silva. The logs were peeled by Abel Pino, who at the time was seventy-eight years old. Charles Pepper supervised construction of the building, and Bert Cheney hauled rocks. Joe Rench and Ray Provine poured the concrete floor, and after Joe's sudden death, his wife, Margaret, supervised a crew

Smokey Bear Museum in Capitan, which opened in 1961. The building was designed by Dorothy Guck from U.S. Forest Service manuals. *Photograph courtesy of David Cunningham, Smokey Bear State Park.*

from Roswell that constructed the fireplace. Arthur Clemens, from Picacho, carved the first Smokey Bear statue in the front of the museum. A second statue was carved by Kevin Woff in 1980 when the first statue was destroyed by a severe windstorm.

The museum opened in 1961 and was filled with Smokey Bear memorabilia. Because of the village's efforts constructing the museum, President Dwight Eisenhower presented Capitan with a golden Smokey Bear statute as the first community in the nation recognized for its conservation efforts. Twelve-year-old Judy Bell went to Washington and accepted the award on behalf of the Village of Capitan.

SMOKEY BEAR STATE PARK

A Smokey Bear State Park was envisioned, and in 1974, Congress passed a resolution that, upon his death, the bear's remains would be returned to Capitan. The New Mexico legislature provided $50,000 in funding, which was matched by the Federal Bureau of Outdoor Recreation. The monument was dedicated on May 15, 1976, with U.S. congressman Harold Runnels, who had done much to establish the park and to bring Smokey back to New Mexico, as the guest speaker.

In 1978, the Village of Capitan donated an additional three acres to the park complex, and Virgil and Millie Wallace donated land for parking. Groundbreaking for the visitors' center took place in May 1978. The park was dedicated on June 21, 1979, and was initially operated by the state parks until the State Forestry Department assumed management in 1990 and total responsibility of the complex in July 1992. The complex includes displays, a small exhibit area, landscaped grounds and interpretive trails with native plants and Smokey Bear's grave.

In 1983, the U.S. Postal Service announced a new Smokey Bear stamp with first-day issue to take place in Washington. After a vigorous local campaign, Postmaster William Bolger relented in February 1984 and announced that the first-day issue would occur at Capitan. On August 23, 1984, Smokey Bear was honored with his own commemorative stamp by the U.S. Postal Service. The presentation by assistant postmaster general Harry C. Penttala took place in Capitan.[161]

In 1994, the nation celebrated the fiftieth anniversary of the bear being designated as the national symbol of fire prevention. That same year, the New Mexico legislature designated July as Smokey Bear Month in Capitan.

In 2000, Capitan celebrated the fiftieth anniversary of the finding of Smokey Bear during the Capitan Gap Fire.

Perhaps the greatest tribute to the little bear cub is the naming of the Forest Service district as the Smokey Bear Ranger District.

NOTES

Preface

1. Terry L. Knight, *Archaeological Survey of Abandoned Coal Mine Locations Near Capitan and White Oaks, New Mexico* (Santa Fe: Museum of New Mexico, Office of Archaeological Studies, 1991), 9–10.
2. French-Canadian Theophilus Lalonde later changed his name to Teofilo LaLone.
3. Electronic mail from Rich Eastwood dated November 21 and 28, 2011.
4. Edward B. Choate, *History of the Capitan Community, 1890–1950* (Masters thesis, Eastern New Mexico University, 1954), 31.

Chapter i

5. George B. Anderson, *History of New Mexico: Its Resources and People, Volume II* (Los Angeles: Pacific States Publishing Company, 1907), 754–55.
6. *Seaborn T. Gray Passes to His Reward*. Obituary of Seaborn Gray dated July 16, 1916, and John A. Haley, ed., *The Yearbook of Lincoln County New Mexico: Descriptive, Historical, Biographical, Statistical, Stock Raising, Mining Agricultural Industrial, Climate, Scenery.* (Carrizozo, NM: The Carrizozo News, 1913), 78.
7. *Lincoln County News,* "Gray Family Reunion Visits Old Homestead," June 17, 2004, 10.
8. Anderson, *History of New Mexico,* 754–55.

9. Knight, *Archaeological Survey,* 24.

10. *Capitan Progress*, October 11, 1901.

11. Robert Leslie, *History of Coal Production in the Sierra Blanca Coal Field.* (N.p., n.d.)

12. Knight, *Archaeological Survey,* 18.

13. Ethel Keathley, "Coalora—The Coal Mining Town," *Lincoln County News*, date unknown, probably 1958.

14. *El Capitan*, September 14, 1900.

15. *Capitan Progress*, January 18, 1901.

16. Knight, *Archaeological Survey,* 18, 20.

17. Ibid., 13.

18. Ibid., 14.

19. Ibid., 15.

20. Ibid., 9, 11.

21. Ibid., 11.

22. Ibid., 16.

23. Ibid., 17.

24. Choate, *History of the Capitan Community*, 78.

25. John W. McPhee, "Family Memories of the Eddy Brothers," in Linne Townsend, ed., *Things Remembered: Alamogordo, New Mexico 1898–1998* (Alamogordo, NM: Alamogordo/Otero County Celebration, 1998.)

26. Knight, *Archaeological Survey,* 11.

27. Ibid., 13.

28. Johnson Stearns, *The Carrizozo Story*, (published privately, December 1987), 14.

29. Johnson Stearns, interview by Gary Cozzens, December 13, 2011.

30. Marci L. Riskin, *The Train Stops Here: New Mexico's Railroad Legacy* (Albuquerque: University of New Mexico Press, 2005), 130–31.

CHAPTER 2

31. Choate, *History of the Capitan Community,* 24.

32. *White Oaks Eagle*, Thursday, May 24, 1900.

33. Herbert Lee Traylor, "Early Capitan," (Unpublished manuscript for the Capitan Woman's Club, January 15, 1980), 6–7.

34. John L. Sinclair, "Mother Julian," *New Mexico Magazine*, March 1990, 45.

35. Dorothy Guck, "Capitan: Happy Home Town," *New Mexico Magazine*. June 1954, 43–45.

36. Hollis Cummins, interview by Gary Cozzens, November 25, 2011.

37. Hyde, Garth. Interview by Gary Cozzens, November 28, 2011.

38. *Capitan Progress*, January 18, 1901.

39. Stearns, *The Carrizozo Story*, 21.

40. Anderson, *History of New Mexico:* 477; and Pearce S. Grove, Becky J. Barnett and Sandra J. Hansen, *New Mexico Newspapers: A Comprehensive Guide to Bibliographical Entries and Locations.* (Albuquerque: University of New Mexico Press, 1975), 247–49.

41. James W. White, *The History of Post Offices in Lincoln County* (Farmington, NM: published privately, April 2007), 22.

42. Ibid., 24–25.

43. Choate, *History of the Capitan Community*, 70.

44. Ibid., 70–71.

45. Traylor, *Early Capitan*, 6.

46. Herbert Lee Traylor, "Capitan Schools: Seventy-five Years 1912–1987." (Unpublished paper, circa 1987).

47. Wally Ferguson, interview by Gary Cozzens, November 27, 2011.

48. *Capitan Progress*, January 18, 1901.

49. Choate, *History of the Capitan Community*, 12.

50. Hollis Cummins, interview by Gary Cozzens, August 28, 2005.

51. Ibid., November 25, 2011.

52. Unpublished interview by Paul Baker for the *Lincoln News*, 1956.

53. Electronic mail from Nancy Hasbrouck, dated July 10, 2011.

54. Ibid.

55. Baker for the *Lincoln News*, 1956.

56. Lionel W. Lippman, and Virginia Watson Jones, *Capitan, New Mexico 1900–2000: Home of Smokey Bear, The Living Symbol* (Roswell, NM: Friends of Smokey—Capitan, Inc., 2000), 42.

57. *Capitan Progress*, July 3, 1903.

58. Baker for the *Lincoln News*, 1956.

59. Choate, *History of the Capitan Community*, 82.

60. Herbert Lee Traylor, *Tales of the Sierra Blanca: Stories of Long Ago* (Roswell, NM: Pioneer Printing Company, Inc., 1983), 1–16. In this chapter Traylor produces a list of known observers of the race. Also Fred LaMay, interview by Barbara Jeanne Reily-Branum in Nogal, September 29, 1995, 12–13.

CHAPTER 3

61. Sinclair, *Mother Julian*, 46–47. The 1910 U.S. census has James and Anna Julian living in Lincoln County, so he would have deserted her after that year.

62. Roberta Haldane, letter to Ann Buffington dated July 22, 1997.

63. Peter White, and Mary Ann White, eds., *Along the Rio Grande: Cowboy Jack Thorp's New Mexico* (Santa Fe, NM: Ancient City Press, 1988), 53–54.

64. Roberta Haldane, letter to Ann Buffington dated July 22, 1997.

65. Sinclair, *Mother Julian*, 49.

66. L.C. Cozzens, interview by Gary Cozzens, November 22, 2011.

67. Sinclair, *Mother Julian*, 47.

68. Ibid., 47.

69. Ibid., 49.

70. "Last Rites for Mrs. Julian Held Sunday," *Lincoln County News*. 26, no. 48. (July 4, 1952).

CHAPTER 4

71. SWCA Environment Consultants, *Hondo Valley Snapshots: Tinnie* (New Mexico Transportation Department, circa 2005), 18.

72. Clarence Hilburn wrote "George Titsworth…when his warehouse and Apple Shed were burned down. He did not show up during the burning, it was a good thing for him because two brothers were waiting for him to show up with cocked guns ready to shoot him. They were not brothers of my grandfather." Clarence S. Hillburn, letter to editor, *Lincoln County News*, dated September 2005. See also *Alamogordo News*, "Titsworth Stock Burned at Capitan," October 18, 1923.

73. Garth Hyde, interview by Gary Cozzens, November 28, 2011.

74. Doyle and L.C. Cozzens, interview by Gary Cozzens, November 22, 2011.

75. Chuck Hornung, "Gunsmoke in Capitan," *Journal of Wild West History* 1, no. 3, (June 2008), 17.

76. *Capitan News*, August 25, 1905.

77. New Mexico Mounted Patrol report of L.F. Arvant dated August 19, 1905. Letters Received, New Mexico Mounted Patrol Reports, New Mexico State Record Center and Archives, Santa Fe, New Mexico.

78. Hornung, "Gunsmoke in Capitan," 20.

79. *Capitan News*, "Left for Beef," August 25, 1905.

80. Bundy Avant as told to Arthur Clements. "The Bundy Avant Story, Part II," *True West* (July–August 1978): 27.

81. Hornung, "Gunsmoke in Capitan," 20.

82. *Capitan News*, "His Troubles Are Ended," August 25, 1905.

83. *Alamogordo News*, September 2, 1905.

84. This public opinion column in an undated and unidentified newspaper was written by "JUSTICIA" in response to George Titsworth being implicated in the death of Robert Hurt. Copy in possession of author.

85. Cecil Bonney, *Looking Over My Shoulder* (Roswell, NM: Hall–Poorbaugh Press, 1971), 162.

86. John A. Haley, ed., *The Yearbook of Lincoln County New Mexico: Descriptive, Historical, Biographical, Statistical, Stock Raising, Mining Agricultural Industrial, Climate, Scenery* (Carrizozo, NM: The Carrizozo News), 1913.

87. Hurt's grandson, Clarence Hilburn, thinks Robert Hurt was the one who reported the Titsworth Company for illegally dispensing prescription drugs. Clarence Hilburn (undated), September 2005 letter to the editor, *Lincoln County News*.

88. Fred LaMay, interview by Barbara Jeanne Reily-Branum in Nogal, September 29, 1995, 13–14.

89. Bonney, *Looking Over My Shoulder*, 162.

90. *The Corona Maverick*, February 2, 1923; and Bonney, *Looking Over My Shoulder*, 166.

91. Bonney, *Looking Over My Shoulder*, 168

92. *Corona Maverick*, May 18, 1923.

93. Bonney, *Looking Over My Shoulder*, 167–68.

94. Sinclair, "Mother Julian," 48; and Bonney, *Looking Over My Shoulder*, 167.

95. Clarence Hilburn, September 2005 letter to the editor, *Lincoln County News*.

Chapter 5

96. Willa Stone, interview by Gary Cozzens, November 26, 2011.

97. Herbert Lee Traylor, *Memoirs of Deseo* (Published privately by H.L. Traylor), 1993.

98. Agatha Long, interview by Gary Cozzens, December 4, 2011.

99. Guy Crandall, *I Rode a Horse Wild and Free* (Published privately by Guy Crandall, 1990), 21–22.

100. Ibid., 41–42.

CHAPTER 6

101. Ruth Rule Smith, *The Golden Rule* (Published privately, about 1985), 38–39.

102. Ibid. 40–41.

103. Pete Mocho, "Pete Mocho on his Family and Life" (Unpublished manuscript, 1971), 3–4.

104. Nora Mocho, "John Mocho" (Unpublished manuscript, n.d.), 5–6.

105. Mocho, "Pete Mocho on his Family and Life," 3–5; Mocho, "John Mocho", 4–7.

106. Truman Spencer Jr., Talk given to the Lincoln County Historical Society on the Carrizozo Bar W and the Block Ranch, March 13, 1974.

107. Carleton Britton, "A Little Britton History," in Pat Garrett, ed., "Traveling Through Time in Capitan, New Mexico" (Capitan Public Library, unpublished manuscript, 2006), 5–6.

108. Ibid., 6.

109. John L. Sinclair, *Cowboy Riding Country.* (Albuquerque: University of New Mexico Press, 1982), 50.

110. Britton, "A Little Britton History," 8–10.

111. *Albuquerque Tribune Online*, "Tackling Block Ranch," August 30, 2004, 3–4.

112. Sinclair, *Cowboy Riding Country*, 51–52.

113. Mark L. Gardner, *Jack Thorp's Songs of the Cowboys Centennial Edition* (Santa Fe: Museum of New Mexico Press, 2005), 29.

114. Ibid., 11; Herb Seckler, *The Ruidoso Countryside: The Early Days* (Published privately, 1987), 38–39.

115. Crandall, *I Rode a Horse Wild and Free*, 56.

CHAPTER 7

116. Patricia M. Spoerl, *A Brief History of the Early Years of the Lincoln National Forest* (Lincoln National Forest, February 1981), 2.

117. Wilfried E. Roeder, "The Ranger at Capitan: Clement Hightower and the Lincoln Forest Reserve" (Unpublished manuscript located at the Lincoln National Forest, U.S. Forest Service, Alamogordo, NM, 1991), 2. This eleven-page paper by a former Lincoln National Forest Ranger presents a magnificent picture of the founding of the Forest Service in the Capitan area.

118. Ibid., 2.

119. Ibid., 2.

120. Ibid., 3.

121. Ibid., 6.

122. Ibid., 6.

123. Ibid., 10.

124. Edwin A. Tucker, *The Early Days: A Sourcebook of Southwestern Region History, Book 3* (Cultural Resources Management Report No. 12, USDA Forest Service Southwestern Region, July 1992).

125. Ibid.

126. Chart of Smokey Bear Ranger District sites produced by Jeanette Coe Browning and Anne Browning circa 1985.

127. Tucker, *The Early Days: Book 1*; Herbert L. Traylor, "Everyone Thought Shoemaker Did It," *Oldtimers' Review* (Summer, 1981); and Herbert L. Traylor, "Did Mister Shoemaker Start the Fire on the Northside?" *Oldtimers' Review* (Autumn, 1981). Unless otherwise noted, information on the Shoemaker Fire comes from these sources.

128. Barbara Wagner, letter to Gary Cozzens dated January 26, 2012.

129. Herbert Lee Traylor has these three in the truck in addition to Strickland for a total of four people. Traylor, "Did Mister Shoemaker Start the Fire," 2.

130. Traylor says the woman was in a car with a child, and she drove off when the Forest Service vehicle stopped. Traylor, "Did Mister Shoemaker Start the Fire," 2.

131. Barbara Wagner, undated letter to Gary Cozzens, January 2012.

132. Mocho, "Pete Mocho on his Family and Life," 5.

133. Traylor, "Did Mister Shoemaker Start the Fire," 2.

134. Ibid., 2.

135. Polly E. Chavez, "Camp Capitan: Educational Camp for Girls," *Tradicion Revista* (Fall 2001), 40.

136. Ibid., 41.

137. Ibid., 39.

138. Ibid., 38–41; Chavez, "Camp Capitan" *Lincoln County News*, 1C.

139. John J. Culley, "World War II and a Western Town: The Internment of the Japanese Railroad Workers of Clovis, New Mexico," *Western History Quarterly* 13, no. 1 (January 1982): 54.

140. P.W. Herrick, "Report on the Raton Ranch, Civilian Detention Station, United States State Department," August 19, 1942.

141. Ibid.

142. Ibid.

143. Culley, "World War II," 54.

144. Ibid., 55–56.

145. Herrick, "Report on the Raton Ranch."

Chapter 8

146. Comments by Erma Crawford and Willa Stone.

147. Willa Stone, interview by Gary Cozzens, November 26, 2011.

148. Ibid.

149. William Clifford Lawther Jr., *Smokey Bear 20252: A Biography* (Alexandria, VA: Lindsay Smith Publishers, 1994), 71–80.

150. Paul Jones, interview by Gary Cozzens, November 29, 2011.

151. Doyle and L.C. Cozzens, interview by Gary Cozzens, November 22, 2011.

152. Lawther, *Smokey Bear 20252*, 81–82.

153. Hollis Cummins, interview by Gary Cozzens, November 25, 2011.

154. Ferguson, interview, November 27, 2011.

155. Doyle and L.C. Cozzens, interview, November 22, 2011.

156. Ferguson, interview, November 27, 2011.

157. Lawther, *Smokey Bear 20252*, 138–39.

158. Ibid., 353–59.

159. Paul Jones, interview, November 29, 2011.

160. Dick Cox, interview by Gary Cozzens, November 26, 2011.

161. White, *The History of Post Offices in Lincoln County*, 25.

BIBLIOGRAPHY

Anderson, George B. *History of New Mexico: Its Resources and People.* Vol. II. Los Angeles: Pacific States Publishing Company, 1907.

Anonymous. "Last Rites for Mrs. Julian Held Sunday." *Lincoln County News* 26, no. 48 (July 4, 1952).

————. "Lincoln County and Mescalero Apache Tribe Honor List: Men from Lincoln County, New Mexico and the Mescalero Apache Tribe that Died in: World War I, Word War II, Korean War and Vietnam War." Draft copy, 2000.

————. "Mother Julian." *Ruidoso News*, May 16, 1947.

————. *Service Record Book of Men and Women of Capitan, New Mexico and Community.* Capitan, NM: Norton Pepper VFW Post 7688, 1946.

Baker, Pal. Unpublished interview with Monroe Howard.1957.

Blackburn, Nancy Cagle. *Pine Lodge, 100 years, 1909–2009.* Privately published, 2009.

Blake, Donna. Electronic mail correspondence on September 15, 2011.

Bonney, Cecil. *Looking Over My Shoulder*. Roswell, NM: Hall-Poorbaugh Press, 1971.

Browning, Jeanette Coe, and Anne Browning. *Chart of Smokey Bear Ranger District Sites*. 1985.

Cave, Dorothy. *Beyond Courage: One Regiment Against Japan, 1941–1945*. Las Cruces, NM: Yucca Tree Press, 1992.

Chavez, Polly E. "Camp Capitan: Educational Camp for Girls." *Tradicion Revista* (Fall 2001).

———. "Camp Capitan." *Lincoln County News*, July 14, 2000.

Choate, Edward B. "History of the Capitan Community, 1890–1950." Masters thesis, Eastern New Mexico University, 1954.

Cox, Dick. Interview by Gary Cozzens on November 26, 2011.

Cozzens, Doyle, and L.C. Cozzens. Interview by Gary Cozzens on November 22, 2011.

Cozzens, Gary, *The Nogal Mesa: A History of Kivas and Ranchers in Lincoln County*. Charleston, SC: The History Press, 2011.

Cozzens, Gary. "The Officers All Got Drunk: The Use of Alcohol at Ft. Stanton." Unpublished manuscript, 2006.

Cozzens, L.C. Interview by Gary Cozzens on October 12 and December 21, 2009, and February 15, 2010.

Crandall, Guy. *I Rode a Horse Wild and Free*. Saline, MI: McNaughton and Gunn, Inc., 1990.

Crawford, Erma. Interview by Gary Cozzens on October 9, 2011.

Culley, John J. "World War II and a Western Town: The Internment of the Japanese Railroad Workers of Clovis, New Mexico." *Western History Quarterly* 13, no. 1. (January 1982).

Cummins, Hollis. Interview by Gary Cozzens on August 28, 2005, and November 25, 2011.

Cummins, Ted. *A Century of Memories*. Published privately, 2000.

Dean, Gerald, Jr. Interview by Gary Cozzens on December 3, 2011.

Dike, Shelton H. *The Territorial Post Offices of New Mexico*. Albuquerque, NM: Published privately by Dr. S.H. Dike, 1958.

Eastwood, Rich. Electronic mail dated November 21 and 28, 2011.

Ferguson, Wally. Interview by Gary Cozzens on November 27, 2011.

Gardner, Mark L. *Jack Thorp's Songs of the Cowboys Centennial Edition*. Santa Fe: Museum of New Mexico Press, 2005.

Garrett, Pat, ed. "Traveling Through Time in Capitan, New Mexico." Capitan Public Library. Unpublished manuscript, 2006.

Griffin, Marcus, and Eva Jane Matson. *Heroes of Bataan*. Las Cruces, NM: Yucca Tree Press, 1989 (first edition by Griffin) and 1994 (second edition by Matson).

Grove, Pearce S., Becky J. Barnett and Sandra J. Hansen. *New Mexico Newspapers: A Comprehensive Guide to Bibliographical Entries and Locations*. Albuquerque: University of New Mexico Press, 1975.

Guck, Dorothy. "Capitan: Happy Home Town." *New Mexico Magazine*. (June 1954): 43–45.

Haldane, Roberta. Letter to Ann Buffington dated July 22, 1997.

———. Letter to Ann Buffington dated August 14, 1997.

———. Letter to Ann Buffington dated August 28, 1997.

———. Letter to Gary Cozzens dated July 10, 2011.

BIBLIOGRAPHY

Haley, John A., ed. *The Yearbook of Lincoln County New Mexico: Descriptive, Historical, Biographical, Statistical, Stock Raising, Mining Agricultural Industrial, Climate, Scenery.* Carrizozo, NM: The Carrizozo News, 1913.

Hasbrouch, Nancy. Electronic mail on July 10, July 11 and September 15, 2011.

Herrick, P.W. "Report on the Raton Ranch, Civilian Detention Station." United States State Department of Justice report dated August 19, 1942.

Hilburn, Clarence S. Letter to editor. *Lincoln County News*, September 2005

———. Letter to Gary Cozzens dated August 5, 2008.

Hornung, Chuck. "Gunsmoke in Capitan." *Journal of Wild West History* 1, no. 3, June 2008, 17–22.

Hyde, Garth. Interview by Gary Cozzens on November 28, 2011.

Jones, Paul. Interview by Gary Cozzens on November 29, 2011.

Julyan, Robert. *The Mountains of New Mexico.* Albuquerque: University of New Mexico Press, 2006.

———. *The Place Names of New Mexico.* Albuquerque: University of New Mexico Press, 1996.

Keathley, Ethel. "Coalora—The Coal Mining Town." *Lincoln County News*, date unknown, probably 1958.

Knight, Terry L. *Archaeological Survey of Abandoned Coal Mine Locations Near Capitan and White Oaks, New Mexico.* Santa Fe: Museum of New Mexico, Office of Archaeological Studies, 1991.

LaMay, Fred. Interview by Barbara Jeanne Reily-Branum in Nogal on September 29, 1995.

Lawther, William Clifford, Jr. *Smokey Bear 20252: A Biography.* Alexandria, VA: Lindsay Smith Publishers, 1994.

Leslie, Robert. *History of Coal Production in the Sierra Blanca Coal Field*. Publisher and date unknown, likely published about 1909.

Lindgren, Waldemar, Louis C. Garton and Charles H. Gordon. "Ore Deposits in New Mexico." Washington, D.C.: Department of the Interior, U.S. Geological Survey, Professional Paper 68. Government Printing Office, 1910.

Lippman, Lionel W., and Virginia Watson Jones. *Capitan, New Mexico 1900–2000: Home of Smokey Bear, The Living Symbol*. Roswell, NM: Friends of Smokey—Capitan, Inc., 2000.

Long, Agatha. Interview by Gary Cozzens on December 4, 2011.

Matson, Eva Jane. *It Tolled for New Mexico*. Las Cruces, NM: Yucca Tree Press, 1994.

McPhee, John W. "Family Memories of the Eddy Brothers." In *Things Remembered: Alamogordo, New Mexico 1898–1998*. Edited by Linnie Townsend. Alamogordo, NM: Alamogordo/Otero County Celebration, 1998.

Melzer, Richard. *Coming of Age in the Great Depression: The Civilian Conservation Corps in New Mexico*. Las Cruces, NM: Yucca Tree Press, 2000.

Mocho, Nora. "John Mocho." Unpublished manuscript, 1971.

Mocho, Pete. "Pete Mocho on his Family and Life." Unpublished Manuscript, date unknown.

Peters, Chloe. *50 Golden Years in Golden Service for the Capitan Nazarenes*. Published privately in 1966.

Peters, LaMoyne, and Opal Jones Peters. Interview by Gary Cozzens on October 12 and December 21, 2009, and November 26, 2011.

Reed, Ollie, Jr. "Tackling the Block Ranch." *Albuquerque Tribune Online*. August 27, 2004.

Riskin, Marci L. *The Train Stops Here: New Mexico's Railway Legacy*. Albuquerque: University of New Mexico Press, 2005.

Roeder, Wilfried E. "The Ranger at Capitan: Clement Hightower and the Lincoln Forest Reserve." Unpublished manuscript located at the Lincoln National Forest, U.S. Forest Service, Alamogordo, NM, 1991.

"Seaborn T. Gray Passes to His Reward." Dated July 16, 1916, copy in possession of the author.

Seckler, Herb. *The Ruidoso Countryside: The Early Days*. Published privately, 1987.

Shields, Helen B., and David T. Kirkpatrick. *A Cultural-Resources Inventory for Project TPM-380-(33)65 Along 43 Miles (69.2 Kilometers) of U.S. Highway 380 Right-of-Way Between Carrizozo and Hondo, Lincoln County, New Mexico*. Tularosa, NM: Human Resources Research, 2001.

Sinclair, John L. *Cowboy Riding Country*. Albuquerque: University of New Mexico Press, 1982.

———. "Mother Julian." *New Mexico Magazine*. March 1990, 44–49.

Smith, Ruth Rule. *The Golden Rule*. Published privately about 1985.

Spencer, Truman, Jr. Talk given to the Lincoln County Historical Society on the Carrizozo Bar W and the Block Ranch. March 13, 1974. Copy held at Lincoln County Historical Society, Lincoln, New Mexico.

Spoerl, Patricia M. "A Brief History of the Early Years of the Lincoln National Forest." Research paper for the Lincoln National Forest, February 1981.

Stearns, Johnson. The Carrizozo Story. Published privately, December 1987.

———. Interview with Gary Cozzens on December 13, 2011.

Stone, Willa. Interview with Gary Cozzens on November 26, 2011.

SWCA Environment Consultants. *Hondo Valley Snapshots: Tinnie*. New Mexico Transportation Department, circa 2005.

Traylor, Herbert Lee. "Did Mister Shoemaker Start the Fire on the Northside?" *Oldtimers' Review* (Autumn 1981).

————. "Early Capitan." Unpublished manuscript for the Capitan Woman's Club, January 15, 1980.

————. "Early History of the Capitan Municipal School System." Unpublished manuscript, 1991.

————. "Everyone Thought Shoemaker Did It." *Oldtimers' Review* (Summer 1981).

————. *Memoirs of DeSeo*. Las Cruces, NM: Vincomp Publications, 1993.

————. *Tales of the Sierra Blanca: Stories of Long Ago*. Roswell, NM: Pioneer Printing Company, Inc., 1983.

Traylor, Herbert L., and Louise Coe Runnels. *The Saga of Sierra Blanca*. Roswell, NM: Old Timers Press, 1986.

Tucker, Edwin A. *The Early Days: A Sourcebook of Southwestern Region History, Book 1*. Cultural Resources Management Report No. 7, USDA Forest Service Southwestern Region, September 1989.

————. *The Early Days: A Sourcebook of Southwestern Region History, Book 3*. Cultural Resources Management Report No. 12, USDA Forest Service Southwestern Region, July 1992.

Wagner, Barbara. Letter to Gary Cozzens. January 2012.

————. Letter to Gary Cozzens. January 26, 2012.

Wegemann, Caroll H. "Geology and Coal Resources of the Sierra Blanca Coal Field, Lincoln and Otero Counties, New Mexico." Contributions to Economic Geology. *U.S. Geological Survey Bulletin* 541 (1914).

White, James W. *The History of Post Offices in Lincoln County*. Farmington, NM: published privately, April 2007.

White, Peter, and Mary Ann White, eds. *Along the Rio Grande: Cowboy Jack Thorp's New Mexico*. Santa Fe, NM: Ancient City Press, 1988.

INDEX

ABOUT THE AUTHOR

A native New Mexican, Gary Cozzens grew up in Portales, where he graduated from Portales High School and Eastern New Mexico University, earning a double major in history and political science. Following graduation, he served in the United States Marine Corps for a total of twenty-four years, including Operation Desert Storm, and retired as a major in 1999. Cozzens is employed by the Region IX Education Cooperative

Photograph by Shirley Crawford.

in Ruidoso, New Mexico. He is a member of the Lincoln County Historical Society, Fort Stanton, Inc., the Lincoln County Site Watch program and the Historical Society of New Mexico. He is the author of *The Nogal Mesa*, also published by The History Press. Gary and his wife, Shirley Crawford, live on the Nogal Mesa in Lincoln County, New Mexico.

Visit us at
www.historypress.net